Top 25 locator map
(continues on inside
back cover)
◄

CityPack
Toronto *Top 25*

MARILYN WOOD

If you have any comments
or suggestions for this guide
you can contact the editor at
Citypack@theAA.com

AA Publishing
Find out more about AA Publishing and the
wide range of services the AA provides by
visiting our website at *www.theAA.com*

About This Book

ORGANIZATION

This guide is divided into six sections:

- Planning Ahead, Getting There
- Living Toronto—Toronto Now, Toronto Then, Time to Shop, Out and About, Walks, Toronto by Night
- Toronto's Top 25 Sights
- Toronto's Best—best of the rest
- Where To—detailed listings of restaurants, hotels, shops and nightlife
- Travel Facts—practical information

In addition, easy-to-read side panels provide extra facts and snippets, highlights of places to visit and invaluable practical advice.

The colors of the tabs on the page corners match the colors of the triangles aligned with the chapter names on the contents page opposite.

MAPS

The fold-out map in the wallet at the back of this book is a comprehensive street plan of Toronto. The first (or only) grid reference given for each attraction refers to this map. **The Top 25 locator map** found on the inside front and back covers of the book itself is for quick reference. It shows the Top 25 Sights, described on pages 26–50, which are clearly plotted by number (**1**–**25**, not page number) across the city. The second map reference given for the Top 25 Sights refers to this map.

Contents

Planning Ahead

WHEN TO GO

The best time to visit Toronto is summer, when Ontario Place, Paramount Canada's Wonderland and all the other attractions open, and the ferries to the islands are in full swing.

Fall is also good. The weather is still warm, and outside the city the forests take on a rich golden glow.

TIME

Toronto is on Eastern Standard Time, three hours ahead of Los Angeles and five hours behind GMT.

AVERAGE DAILY MAXIMUM TEMPERATURES

JAN	FEB	MAR	APR	MAY	JUN	JUL	AUG	SEP	OCT	NOV	DEC
23°F	26°F	35°F	47°F	57°F	68°F	70°F	70°F	64°F	53°F	42°F	30°F
-4°C	-3°C	1°C	8°C	14°C	19°C	21°C	21°C	18°C	12°C	6°C	-1°C

Spring (mid-March to late May) is unpredictable. Occasional snow or ice storms occur as late as mid-April.

Summer (early June to late August) is warm to hot, with occasional rain or humidity and cooler evenings.

Fall (September to October) has cooler temperatures, sunny days and occasional rain; the weather makes for ideal exploring.

Winter (November to March) can be harsh. November is always unpredictable and mid-winter is much colder because of the unrelenting winds blowing off Lake Ontario.

WHAT'S ON

February *Winterfest*: Winter extravaganza with top-notch skaters and entertainers.
March *Canadian Music Festival*.
St. Patrick's Day Parade (17 March).
May *Milk International Children's Festival* (➤ 59) (☎ 416/973-3000).
June *Toronto International Dragon Boat Race Festival*: Chinese festival where colorful dragon boats feature.
Downtown Jazz Festival: Jazz performed at various venues throughout the city (☎ 416/928-2033).

July *Fringe of Toronto Theatre Festival*: Local, national and international acts (☎ 416/966-1062).
Canada Day Celebration (1 Jul): Canada's birthday is celebrated with entertainers and firework displays.
Caribana Carnival: North America's largest Caribbean carnival; costumes, parades and music citywide (☎ 416/465-4884).
August *Canadian National Exhibition and International Air Show*: Agricultural fair alongside pop entertainment and an air show

(☎ 416/393-6000).
Toronto International Film Festival (☎ 416/967-7371).
November *Royal Agricultural Winter Fair and Royal Horse Show*: Agricultural exhibits and equestrian events (☎ 416/263-3400)..
December *Cavalcade of Lights*: Thousands of lights illuminate the central square; skating parties and other events finish with New Year celebrations.
First Night Celebration of the Arts: New Year's Eve indoor celebration of the arts (☎ 416/973-3000).

4

TORONTO ONLINE

www.torontotourism.com
Toronto's official tourist website is run by the Toronto Visitors and Convention Bureau. Shopping, accommodations, attractions, theater and restaurants.

www.toronto.com
A comprehensive Toronto guide. Good event and concert listings, shopping information, plus excellent links.

www.city.toronto.on.ca
The City of Toronto's comprehensive attractions guide, with much history and archival photographs.

www.wheretoronto.com
Practical info and up-to-date event listings.

www.fyitoronto.com
Breaking Toronto news stories.

www.ontariotravel.net
The Ontario's official travel information site.

www.discoverniagara.com
Niagara Tourism's official site.

www.niagaraparks.com
Niagara region tourist information focusing on accommodations and attractions.

www.theatreintoronto
The Toronto Theatre Alliance site lists all the live theater, dance, ballet, opera, comedy and musical theater companies in Toronto, with info about half-price tickets.

www.ttc.ca
Toronto Transit Commission site, with details on buses, subways and streetcars.

www.findtheway.ca
Information on transit systems for the city and outlying areas.

GOOD TRAVEL SITES

www.fodors.com
A complete travel-planning site. Book air tickets, cars and rooms; research prices and weather; pose questions to fellow travelers; and find links to other sites.

www.worldweb.com
A comprehensive travel guide. Plan your trip aided by online hotel booking, info about transportation; weather; restaurants; events and shopping. Maps and photo gallery.

CYBERCAFÉS

Insomnia Internet Café
✉ 563 Bloor Street West
☎ 416/588-3807;
www.insomniacafe.com
🕐 Mon–Thu 4pm–2am, Fri 4pm–4am, Sat 10am–4am, Sun 10–2am
💷 $10 per hour

Ciber Village Internet Café
✉ 449 Church Street
☎ 416/928-6060;
www.cibervillage.com
🕐 Mon–Sat 10am–10pm, Sun 12pm–8pm 💷 15c per minute

Chapters Café
✉ 110 Bloor Street West
☎ 416/249-9892
🕐 8am–midnight 💷 $5 per hour

Getting There

ENTRY REQUIREMENTS

Citizens of EU and most British Commonwealth countries require a valid passport and return or onward ticket but no visa. US citizens must show proof of permanent residency (government-issued photo ID). People under 18 must have a parent or guardian letter stating a length of stay.

MONEY

The Canadian dollar is the unit of currency (= 100 cents). Coins include 1¢ (penny), 10¢ (dime) and 25¢ (quarter), and $1 (loonie) and $2 (twoonie). Bills (notes) are in $5, $10, $20, $50 and $100. Stores may refuse large bills.

$10

$20

$50

$100

ARRIVING

Pearson International Airport lies northwest of Toronto, about 17 miles (27km) from the city center. There are three terminals; the airport is undergoing a major reconstruction and flights are shifted from one terminal to the next, but most international flights arrive at Trillium 3.

FROM PEARSON INTERNATIONAL AIRPORT

For information on Pearson Airport ☎ Terminals 1 and 2, 905/676-3506; Terminal 3, 416/776-5100. Approved airport taxis and limos to greater Toronto leave from the arrivals level of each terminal. Fare is determined by zone; arrange it in advance with dispatcher or driver. To downtown the cost is Can$40–50. Journey time is usually 30–40 minutes.

Airport Express Bus (☎ 905/564-3232 or 905/564-6333) serves downtown hotels and Bay Street Bus terminal. Between 1am and 5am a bus runs every two hours, and then every 30 minutes; buy tickets from the driver (cost Can$14.25; journey time about 30–45 minutes). The airport is also served by public buses and subways. The Toronto Transit Commission (TTC) operates buses between the airport and Kipling subway station every 20 minutes. daily 5.30am–12.30am; stops are at Kipling station, Dundas Street and East Mall Crescent, Terminal 3 and Terminal 2.

ARRIVING BY CAR

The US highway system leads directly into Canada. From Michigan, you enter at Detroit-

Subway

Windsor via I-75 and the Ambassador Bridge or Port Huron-Sarnia via I-94 and the Bluewater Bridge. From New York State, using I-90 you can enter at Buffalo-Fort Erie; Niagara Falls, NY-Niagara Falls; or Niagara Falls, NY-Lewiston, Using I-81, you can cross at Hill Island; using Route 37, you cross either at Ogdensburg-Johnstown or Rooseveltown-Cornwall. Once across the border, you approach Toronto from the west by the Queen Elizabeth Way or Highway 401, from the east by Highway 2 or Highway 401. You need your driver's license, car registration and proof of car insurance. Boston is 65 miles (910km from Toronto); Buffalo 96 miles (154km); Chicago 533 miles (859km); New York 606 miles (976km).

ARRIVING BY BUS

Greyhound Canada (☎ 416/594–1010; 800/ 661–8747) and commuter buses arrive at the Metro Coach Terminal (☎ 416/393–7911) at 610 Bay Street near Dundas.

ARRIVING BY TRAIN

GO Transit commuter trains (☎ 416/869–3200) and Amtrak (☎ 800/872-7245 in the US) and VIA Rail (☎ 888/842-7245; www.viarail.ca in Canada) long-distance trains arrive at Union Station, which is linked directly to the subway.

GETTING AROUND

The subway is fast, quiet, clean and easy to use. You need a token (5 for Can$10 or single fare Can$2.25), which can be bought in any subway station. Drop it into the box at the ticket window or into the turnstile. To ride buses and streetcars you need a transfer (available from the red machines in subway stations or from the streetcar or bus driver) a token or exact change. Bus stops are at or near corners and are marked by elongated signs with red stripes and bus and streetcar diagrams. Pick up a Ride Guide map at subway stations. Cabs can be hailed on the street.

For more information on getting around ► 91–92.

INSURANCE

Make sure your policy covers accidents, medical expenses, personal liability, trip cancellation and interruption, delayed departure and loss or theft of personal property. If you plan to rent a car, check your insurance covers you for collision, personal accident liability and theft or loss.

DRIVING IN TORONTO

The city speed limit is 30mph (48kph), and right turns are permitted unless posted otherwise. Seat belts are compulsory. Towing is among parking penalties. Get an International Driving Permit if you want to rent a car and you are not a US citizens.

VISITORS WITH DISABILITIES

The subway is not accessible, but the city runs a special service, Wheel-Trans, for which visitors can register (☎ 416/393-4111). Parking privileges are extended to drivers who have disabled plates or a pass allowing parking in "No Parking" zones. For more on visitors with disabilities ► 91.

Living
Toronto

Toronto Now

Above: *Police on bicycles in College Street*
Above right: *College Street, in Little Italy*
Right: *East half of* The Audience, *Skydome*

Toronto used to be a city where the sidewalks were empty by 8pm and the stores were shuttered on Sundays. Some people called it Toronto the Good; today these same scoffers wouldn't recognize it. The city is multicultural and multiethnic with a population of more than 4.5 million originating from a staggering 170 nations and speaking around 100 different languages. And all these ethnic groups seem to get along while retaining their unique cultures—it's more a

---

HISTORIC STREET NAMES

● Toronto's street names recall many prominent families. Jarvis Street is named after William Jarvis, a New England loyalist who became Provincial Secretary, and Beverley Street remembers Virginia loyalist John Beverley, who, age 22, became Attorney General, and was later Chief Justice of Upper Canada, as the region was formally known for many years.

mosaic of cultures and languages than a melting pot. Street signs are commonly in English and in the predominant language of the neighborhood, and weekly and daily newspapers are published in a myriad of languages. This new Toronto is vibrant, cosmopolitan and bursting with energy. Downtown, you will discover a mixture of historic and contemporary architecture—solid Romanesque-revival masterpieces contrasting with skyscrapers and handsome Victorian residences. The city is the second-largest live-theater venue on the continent after New York. Toronto even has a pennant-winning baseball team, the Blue Jays.

In January 1998, the six communities that formerly made up the Municipality of Metroplitan Toronto—which itself was created in 1953 to help alleviate growing pains faced by the community with the rapid increase in immigration following the end of World War II—

Above: *Kensington Market*
Left: *Roy Thomson Hall*

KING OF KENSINGTON

● Canada's most popular TV series, *King of Kensington*, starring Al Waxman and filmed in the mid-1970s, put Kensington Market on the map. On Waxman's death in 2001 the community erected a full-size bronze statue of "The King" and put two bronze benches in Dennison Square—on the corner of Bellevue and Wales avenues—and the area has become a popular spot for picnics.

Above: *Gretzky's Bar in Windsor Street*
Above right: *Art Gallery of Ontario*
Far right: *Cabbagetown*

VITAL STATISTICS

• Toronto is the largest city in Canada and the fifth largest city region in North America.
• At 44° north latitude, Toronto is farther south than Paris, London and even US cities such as Portland and Seattle.
• There are more than 130 golf courses within a 30-minute drive of downtown Toronto.
• The city has more than 6,000 restaurants of which nearly half are ethnic.

became one large megacity known as City of Toronto. You will still find reminders of the pre-megacity communities—Toronto, Etobicoke, North York, Scarborough, York and East York—on shop signs, as part of postal addresses, and in the names of subway stations and newly established Civic Service Centres.

Toronto's culinary landscape is painted in broad brushstrokes that shift and evolve. The city feels the ripple effect of world events as borders change, people scatter and immigration flourishes. Recipes travel freely and suddenly, on main streets, restaurants offer the traditional dishes from distant new lands. Toronto's abundant fresh produce, once exclusively filtered through French, British and Italian cooking techniques, now benefits from the intoxicating spicing of Southeast Asia, the sweet and pungent flavors of the Middle East, and the robust sensibilities of Latin America. It is highly likely that no matter what country you call home, you'll find home cooking in Toronto.

Toronto is the capital of the performing arts scene in English-speaking Canada. The visual

arts scene has blossomed with the opening of some dazzling new venues and the refurbishing of some magnificent old ones. The burgeoning film industry has made nightlife a lot more glamorous as well. Fueling this arts explosion was a massive immigration from culturally nourished countries of Eastern and Central Europe, as well as from England; a growing sense of independence from the mother country; a recognition that if Canadians did not

FIGHT FOR SURVIVAL

• Some 600 artists, teachers and aging activists live on idyllic Algonquin and Ward's Islands, occupying modest cottages and getting by with few amenities and no cars. Their survival is the outcome of a dramatic struggle. In 1956 the local government decided to evict the residents and convert the islands into parkland. Bulldozers moved in and 600 buildings were flattened, but when attempts were made to remove the last enclave, the residents formed a phalanx against the onslaught, placing their children in front. A bitter court fight ended in 1992, when the islanders were granted the right to purchase 99-year leases to their properties.

TORONTO'S FAMOUS

• Toronto gave us classical pianist Glenn Gould, the outrageous Barenaked Ladies, contemporary country Blue Rodeo and current pop stars Shania Twain, Avril Lavigne and Alanis Morrissette. The city is often the backdrop in the novels by Margaret Atwood and in the films from directors Atom Egoyan and David Cronenberg. *Star Trek* actor William Shatner is from Toronto, as are Mike Myers, the comic genius behind Austin Powers, and the talented Jim Carrey.

13

Above: *Café on the observation deck of the CN Tower*
Above right: *Ward's Island Ferry, Toronto Islands*
Far right: *Chinatown*

develop their own arts, then the United States would do it for them; and a growing civic and cultural maturity.

Because of the many movies that have been shot here in recent years, Toronto has also garnered the nickname Hollywood North. It is one of the largest movie and television production centers in North America—in fact, it is third after Los Angeles and New York. Toronto is also the second largest exporter of television programing. The movie and TV industry contributed $1.1 billion to Ontario's economy in 2000, thanks to the availability of excellent crews, the savings from the exchange rate

HONEST ED

• Ed Mirvish is one of Toronto's great impresarios and a living legend. It was the discount store Honest Ed's that brought him fame and fortune. Always a theater lover, he bought the Royal Alexandra in 1963 and converted surrounding warehouses into restaurants. In 1982, when the owners of London's Old Vic were seeking buyers to save the theater, Ed audaciously outbid Andrew Lloyd Webber. He was awarded the prestigious CBE honor by the Queen for his achievements. With his son, David, he built Toronto's Princess of Wales Theatre, which opened in 1993.

between US and Canadian dollars and the variety of locations (Toronto has posed for everything from Paris to Vietnam). The 2003 Oscar-winning *Chicago*, with Catherine Zeta-Jones, Renée Zellweger and Richard Gere as well as *My Big Fat Greek Wedding* with Nia Vardalos, plus the television series *Queer as Folk* with Sharon Gless, were all shot on the city's streets and film stages. September's Toronto International Film Festival, second in stature to Cannes, has become North America's most important film festival among the industry bigwigs, critics and the public.

Meanwhile, despite rapid growth and change, Toronto has managed to preserve a gentle demeanour and feel for tradition, and the city has also retained a strong sense of community. The streets are clean and safe and the public facilities are excellent. Toronto has meta-morphosed into a great world city, where colorful ethnic enclaves converge with imposing banks and government buildings—this is a wonderful place to explore. Nowadays, Toronto, no longer just "the Good," is no less than "absolutely fabulous."

DESIGN EXCHANGE

● A delightful example of Moderne design, a later and more austere version of Art Deco, this Bay Street building is clad in pink granite and smooth buff limestone, and has wonderful stainless-steel doors. Between 1937 and 1983, the DX, as it's now known, was the home of the Toronto Stock Exchange. In 1994 the building reopened as a center devoted to Canadian design. The old trading floor is now used for rotating exhibits.

Toronto Then

Above: *Exhibit on the history of humankind, Royal Ontario Museum*
Above right: *Four-poster bed in Campbell House*

REBELLION

The first mayor of Toronto, William Lyon Mackenzie, shared immigrant aspirations for political reform and campaigned vehemently against the narrow-minded, exclusive power of the Family Compact—a group of ardent British loyalists who controlled the city's economy and politics. By 1837 he was advocating open rebellion, and on 5 December around 700 rebels assembled at Montgomery's Tavern. Led by Mackenzie, they marched on the city. The sheriff called out the militia, who scattered the rebels at Carlton Street. Mackenzie fled to the United States. Two other ringleaders were hanged.

1720 France sets up a trading post at Toronto.

1715 Fort Rouille is built.

1763 The Treaty of Paris secures Canada for Britain.

1787 The British purchase land from the Mississauga tribe on which Toronto will be sited.

1793 John Graves Simcoe, Governor of Upper Canada, arrives and names settlement York.

1813 Americans invade, destroy Fort York, and burn Parliament Buildings.

1834 The city is named Toronto ("meeting place"). William Lyon Mackenzie becomes the first mayor.

1837 Former mayor, Mackenzie, leads a rebellion against the Family Compact (► panel).

1844 George Brown founds *The Globe*.

1858 The Toronto Islands are created from a peninsula smashed by a violent storm.

1867 Canadian Confederation: Toronto becomes capital of Ontario province.

1884	The streets are lit by electricity.
1914–18	70,000 Torontonians enlist and 13,000 are killed in World War I.
1920	The Group of Seven hold their first art exhibition (➤ 27).
1923	The Chinese Exclusion Act restricts Chinese immigration.
1933	The Depression leads to 30 percent unemployment.
1950	Sunday sports are permitted.
1953	Metro organized.
1992/3	Blue Jays win the World Series
1995	The progressive Conservative Government is elected and focuses on budget cuts.
1996	*Fortune* magazine names Toronto "Best City for Work and Family outside the US."
1998	Toronto's six municipalities are merged.
2002/3	Toronto Transit commission opens its third subway line, the Sheppard Line, which connects the former city of North York to downtown Toronto.

Above left: Ancient Inuit painting, The Shaman's Wife, in the Kleinsburg Museum
Above: Nineteenth century British military uniform modelled in front of a cannon during a display at Toronto's Fort York

BUILDING TORONTO

1844 First City Hall
1845 King's College
1851 St. Lawrence Hall
1852 The Toronto Stock Exchange
1869 Eaton's
1886 The Provincial Parliament buildings
1907 The Royal Alexander
1912 The Royal Ontario Museum
1931 Maple Leaf Gardens arena
1965 New City Hall
1971 Ontario Place
1972 Harbourfront development
1975 CN Tower
1989 SkyDome stadium
1993 CBC Building.

Time to Shop

Below: BCE Building
Below right: Queens Quay terminal, Harbourfront

Most of the world's top names in fashion have found a home in Toronto, particularly on the "mink mile" (Bloor Street between Avenue Road and Yonge Street). Chanel, Max Mara, Hermes,

A GOOD SMOKE

Canada has never severed diplomatic or trade relations with Cuba, and so just about every tobacconist in Toronto has a humidor full of Havanas—something you won't find anywhere south of the US border. But if you'll be crossing into the US anytime soon, smoke those stogies in Canada: US laws embargo trade with Cuba, and trying to take goods across the border could lead to charges.

Gucci, Prada, Versace, to name a few, have seasonal windows. Diamonds, watches and crystal sparkle at Tiffany's, Royale de Versailles, Watchcraft and Swarovski. The Canadian flagship store of Roots, a giant in casual clothing and sportswear, occupies a multilevel space and Zara, Latin America's stylish budget-conscious entry in the fashion field, are here as well. Still at the heart of Bloor Street is Holt Renfrew, a three-story style emporium for men, women and the home.

Bloor Street is not the only game in town. On Spadina Avenue around Dundas, fur and garment manufacturers have showrooms and retail outlets. There are Pan-Asian Shopping Malls in Markham and Scarborough that will feel like something in a major city in Asia. Toronto's art and crafts communities show their works on Queen's Street West. The street abounds with custom jewelers, sophisticated glass sculpture galleries and native and Inuit art. Davenport Road at Avenue is the place for classy antiques.

Toronto is proud of its musicians and entertainers, and the huge HMV store on Yonge Street not only has listening stations but also stages live in-store performances. Most Toronto

Eaton Centre

music stores dedicate shelves to Ontario-bred talent such as Shania Twain, Alanis Morrissette, Avril Lavigne and Bryan Adams.

At Queen's Quay Terminal the unique Tilley Endurables Boutique features the infamous Tilley Hat. Advertised as having been retrieved intact after being eaten by an elephant, it comes with a lifetime guarantee and owner's manual. Hudson's Bay Company, a former Upper Canada fur trading post that's as old as Canada itself, and is now familiarly known simply as The Bay, is a major department store selling everything from fur garments to major appliances, electronics and fashions. Stores are on Queen and Bay and Bloor and Yonge, as well as in surburban shopping malls.

Don't miss the biggest sale day of the year, the first business day after Christmas. Most everything in the city, including furs, is half price. Summer sales start in late June and continue through August.

UNDERGROUND CITY

When it's freezing outside, Torontonians appreciate downtown Toronto's vast maze of subterranean tunnels. Here, some 1,100 stores—mostly the usual assortment of chain stores—and cafés burrow between and underneath office towers. The network runs roughly from the Royal York Hotel near Union Station north to the Atrium on Bay and from Park Road, east of Bloor and Yonge, to Bellair Street and the ManuLife Centre.

Out and About

WALKING TOURS

Taste of the World
Shirley Lum's tours include stops in shops, temples, small factories and restaurants. She also operates bycicle tours.
☎ 416/923-6813

Heritage Toronto
Summer walking tours
☎ 416/392-6827

HARBOR TOURS

Great Lakes Schooner Company
Two-hour cruises on a three-masted schooner.
☎ 416/260-6355

Toronto Tours
Glass-enclosed boats cruise the harbor and islands, leaving from Queen's Quay West.
☎ 416/869-1372

INFORMATION

STRATFORD
Distance 93miles (150km)
Journey Time 1.5 hours
🚍 Public Transit
Greyhound (☎ 416/367-8747) to Kitchener then Cha-Co Trails (☎ 519/681-2861) to Stratford.
🚆 VIA Rail (☎ 416/366-8411) to Stratford.
ℹ️ 88 Wellington Street (☎ 519/271-5140).

ORGANIZED SIGHTSEEING

The easy way to orient yourself is to board one of the buses operated by Grayline Tours (☎ 416/594-3310). For a more exciting view, try a seven-minute helicopter tour given by National Helicopters (☎ 905/893-2727). For an

offbeat experience take a Hippo tour aboard an amphibious vehicle (☎ 416/703-4476). For an insight into the workings of the Canadian Broadcasting Corporation and a stroll around the sets of some top comedy shows, take the network's tour (► 62). CHUM/Citytv tours give you a hipper experience of what goes on behind the scenes (► 62).

EXCURSIONS
STRATFORD

Stratford is an attractive Victorian town with good stores, a riverfront park and several good restaurants. There are swans on the Avon River and Shakespeare productions from mid-May to mid-November in three theaters at the Stratford Theatre Festival, which numbers many a famous thespian among its alumni. You can sometimes enjoy discussions with actors and directors and take backstage tours. Nearby, visit the town of Shakespeare for its antiques stores and St. Mary's for its Victorian architecture, and the sprawling city of Kitchener-Waterloo, home of an Oktoberfest and a thriving Saturday Mennonite farmers' market.

NIAGARA FALLS

This natural wonder of the world is on most visitors' itineraries. The Canadian side of the falls gives a far superior view to the American; the 35-mile (56-km) long Niagara Parkway winds along the Niagara River from Chippawa to

Niagara-on-the-Lake past orchards, wineries, parks and picnic areas—a joy for biking and hiking. The area around the falls, especially near Clifton Hill, is spotted with kitschy commercial outlets, but the falls are nonetheless magnificent, even in winter. Don't miss the Maid of the Mist boat ride, which departs from the bottom of Clifton Hill. About 5 miles (8km) north along the Niagara Parkway is the Niagara Parks Botanical Gardens, which includes a butterfly conservatory.

NIAGARA-ON-THE-LAKE

Niagara-on-the-Lake is one of the prettiest and best-preserved 19th-century villages in North America. During the Shaw Festival every year from mid-April to October, the town arranges a series of plays written by George Bernard Shaw and his contemporaries. Away from the festival, you can stroll along Queen Street, visit Fort George National Historic Park, take a jet boat down the Niagara River to get a close-up of the Niagara Gorge, or take in one of the nearby wineries—many have their own restaurants as well as offer wine tastings and tours. The Welland Canal and the village of Jordan are also nearby.

Far left: Tour boat at Queens Quay
Left: Maid of the Mist

INFORMATION

NIAGARA FALLS
Distance 81 miles (130km)
Journey Time 1.5 hours
🚌 Public Transit
Greyhound (☎ 416/367-8747 or 800/661-8747).
🛈 Niagara Falls Canada Visitor and Convention Bureau (✉ 5515 Stanley Avenue ☎ 905/356-6061).
The Niagara Parks Commission (✉ PO Box 150, 7400 Portage Road South ☎ 905/356-2241).
Maid of the Mist (☎ 905/358-5781 🕐 Apr–Oct).
Botanical Gardens (☎ 905/358-0025 🕐 Daily, times vary).

INFORMATION

NIAGARA-ON-THE-LAKE
Distance 81 miles (130km)
Journey Time 1.5 hours
🚌 Public Transit
Greyhound (☎ 416/367-8747 or 800/661-8747) to St. Catharine's then Laidlaw Transit (☎ 905/688-9600).
🚆 VIA Rail (☎ 416/366-8411 or 1/800-561-8630) to St. Catharine's or Niagara Falls.
🛈 Niagara-on-the-Lake Chamber of Commerce (✉ Box 1043, 26 Queen Street ☎ 905/468-4263).

21

Walks

THE SIGHTS

- CN Tower (► 37)
- CBC Building (► 62)
- Metro Hall (► 61)
- Princess of Wales Theatre (► 61)
- Queen Street (► 53, 72)

Roy Thomson Hall

DOWNTOWN HIGHLIGHTS

Walk east from the CN Tower along Front Street to check out the lobby-studios and museum of the CBC Building. Backtrack along Front and turn right up John Street to King. Drop into the Metro Hall for general information and to see the public art, then cross King Street to see the Frank Stella murals in the Princess of Wales Theatre. Cruise east past the Royal Alexandra

Theatre. On the south side of King at Simcoe Street don't miss flying-saucer-like Roy Thomson Hall. Continue on King to York Street and the Exchange Tower, site of the Canadian Sculpture Society's gallery and the Toronto Stock Exchange; at King and Bay streets rises Mies van der Rohe's Toronto Dominion Centre. For an architectural contrast drop into the grand banking hall of the Canadian Imperial Bank of Commerce on King and Yonge. Backtrack to Bay and turn south to Royal Bank Plaza and, across from it, the entrance to the BCE Building, site of the Hockey Hall of Fame. Continue east along Front to the St. Lawrence Centre for the Arts. Note the unusual structure of the Flatiron or Gooderham building in the center of Front. Cross Church Street and keep walking to the St. Lawrence Market (► 47). Backtrack to Church and turn north to King and St. James' Cathedral (► 56). From the Cathedral walk west on King to Bay. Turn north for Old City Hall, then west on Queen and the New City Hall, fronted by an expansive square. Queen leads west past Osgoode Hall, Campbell House and the retro stores farther on.

INFORMATION

Distance 1.1 miles (1.9km)
Time 1.5 hours
Start Point CN Tower
🚇 J9
🚊 Union
End Point Queen Street West at Spadina
🚇 H8
🚋 Queen Street West streetcar

Midtown Hits

Turn your back to the façade of the Ontario Provincial Parliament Buildings, walk south to College Street and turn right. At King's College Road take another right and walk through the University of Toronto campus. Take King's College Circle west to Tower Road. En route, on your left will be University College opposite the Stewart Observatory. Proceed north to Hart House (➤ 35, 56), pause for a meal at Hart House Restaurant, and then visit Soldier's Memorial Tower. Turn right along Hoskin Avenue to Trinity College and then walk east towards Queen's Park. Go left on Avenue Road, going north past the Royal Ontario Museum and the George R. Gardiner Museum. Turn right on fashionable Bloor Street, then head left on Yonge Street to Cumberland Street and walk west. You are now in Yorkville, Toronto's trendy shopping area. Turn down Old York Lane to Yorkville Avenue. Cross Yorkville and go down

Yorkville Avenue, Yorkville

Hazelton Lane to the Hazelton Lanes Complex, where contemporary designer stores can be found, alongwith the vast Whole Foods Market—a superb organic food emporium. Come back out the way you went in and browse through the galleries on Hazelton Avenue. Backtrack to Yorkville Avenue and go left along it to Bay Street; cross Bay. Note the old Firehall and the Yorkville Public Library, both on the left. Continue to Yonge. Turn right and cross the street to the Metro Library and walk south to the Bloor-Yonge subway stop.

INFORMATION

Distance 1.8 miles (2.9km)
Time 2 hours
Start point ★ Ontario Parliament Buildings
🚇 J7
🚉 Queen's Park
End point Bloor/Yonge streets
🚇 K6
🚉 Bloor-Yonge

Toronto by Night

Above: *The city at night seen from the roof of Park Hyatt*
Above right: *The Skydome at night*

THEATRE DISTRICT

Since the mid-19th century, the area now known as the Theatre District has been animated with music halls, theaters and entertainment palaces. The opening of the Royal Alexandra Theatre (► 81, panel) in 1907 breathed new life into the area. In 1989 the new SkyDome stadium brought crowds of up to 55,000 people into the district for baseball games and other events. Restaurants and entertainment spots began springing up overnight, and the pace hasn't stopped. Each street in the Theatre District has its own flavor. Some funky and crowded with shops; some lined with theaters; others are home to massive, 3-story nightclubs.

DOWNTOWN, DOWNTOWN

One of the unique traits of Toronto is that people actually live downtown, and the area is quite safe, whether you're hopping from club to bar or when traveling on the city's extensive subway system. Nestled between skyscrapers and parking lots are many old warehouses converted to living, dining and, of course, dancing spaces, and all are closely linked by foot, taxi or public transit, so there's very little need for a car at night.

CLUBS, CLUBS AND MORE CLUBS

The club-lined streets of downtown Toronto are filled until dawn. Many of the city's dance clubs are on the Richmond Street strip just south of Queen West, which is in itself home to a number of the live-music venues. The College Street area is also a good bet for searching out up-and-coming dance bars, though the area, with its many cafés and bistros, is more oriented toward a laid-back lounge crowd. When the clubs close (by 3am) the fearless night-owls seek out all night raves that you can find out about only by word of mouth.

THE DOCKS

An alternative to the downtown scene is the Docks (► 84, panel) entertainment complex. The Docks is in a class by itself, with the city's most complete array of entertainment, including Toronto's largest lakeside patio, a concert equipped nightclub, and all sorts of outdoor amusements and activities, even a drive-in movie theater.

TORONTO's
top 25 sights

The sights are shown on the maps on the inside front cover and inside back cover, numbered **1**–**25** across the city

Royal Botanical Gardens

HIGHLIGHTS

- Lilacs, magnolias and rhododendrons in the Arboretum
- Bearded iris and peonies in Laking Garden
- Spring bulbs in the Rock Garden
- 20 miles (32km) of trails
- Hedge collection

INFORMATION

- Off map to southwest; Locator map off A1
- 680 Plains Road West, Burlington. Take Queen Elizabeth Way to Hwy 403 (Hamilton). Exit at Hwy 6 North and follow signs to Royal Botanical Gardens Centre
- 905/527-1158; www.rbg.ca
- Outdoor gardens daily 9.30–dusk. Mediterranean Garden daily 9–5. Closed Jan 1
- Café 905/529-2920
- Very good
- Moderate, inexpensive in winter
- Festivals throughout year–lilac, cherry blossom, rose, iris, herb…

If you are wondering what hedge to plant, come and view the 120 varieties in this 2,690-acre (1,090-ha) botanical garden exhibiting 40,000 plants. A bonus is the nature sanctuaries linked by 20 miles (32km) of trails.

Colors and scents The Mediterranean Greenhouse in RBG Centre is at its best from January to May when bougainvillea, jasmine, mimosas, oranges, lemons and spring bulbs all bloom. Annuals blossom in the Hendrie Park garden from June to October along with 3,000 roses. Hendrie's specialty gardens include a shade garden and others devoted to scented and medicinal plants. The Laking Garden has perennials, more than 500 varieties of iris, herbaceous and tree peonies (both the iris and peony flower in June) and a heritage garden. The Rock Garden, with its ponds and waterfalls, dazzles in spring when 125,000 bulbs burst into bloom, followed by flowering cherries. June brings a brilliant display of azaleas. Enjoy this garden from the terrace of the Tea House restaurant.

Trees and wilderness The Arboretum shelters 800 varieties of lilac in the romantic lilac dell—one of the largest collections anywhere—with magnolias, dogwoods and rhododendrons adding to the magnificence. Those hedges are here, as well as an A-to-Z "library" of shrubs, a local wild flower garden and a sea of Ontario trees and shrubs. At the Teaching Garden observe how to create different environments in a small back garden, smell the fragrances of herbs and consider edible ornamentals. The gardens protect a wilderness of high cliffs, ravines and wetlands where deer forage, foxes and coyotes hunt, and blue herons fish. Sanctuaries include Hendrie Valley, Rock Chapel and Cootes Paradise.

McMichael Collection

The artists known as the Group of Seven took their easels north and painted what they saw, revealing the northern wilderness to the rest of the world. Their revolutionary works are now displayed in a woodland setting.

Artist by artist The permanent collection chronicles the development of the Group of Seven. The works of each artist are hung together so that viewers can see how the individuals evolved. All the favorites are here: the brilliantly colored canvases of Lake Superior by Alexander Young Jackson; Algonquin Park as seen by Tom Thomson; the rural villages depicted by Alfred Joseph Casson; the Killarney Provincial Park rendered by Franklin Carmichael; the starkly beautiful icebergs captured by Lawren Harris; portraits of British Columbia by Frederick Horsman Varley; and the portrayal of northwestern forests and Native Canadian villages by Emily Carr. Less familiar followers of the school include John William Beatty, Charles Comfort, George Pepper, Kathleen Daly, Lilias Torrence Newton and Thoreau MacDonald. In one gallery, a series of paintings portrays the Seven working outdoors. The most appealing depicts Franklin Carmichael sketching at Grace Lake in 1935. It shows him from behind perching in front of an easel wrapped in a heavy parka.

First Nations and Inuit art Paintings, drawings, prints and sculptures by contemporary Native American and Inuit artists—Norval Morrisseau, Daphne Odjig, Alex Janvier, Bill Reid—are displayed in changing shows drawn from the gallery's permanent collection. Fine Inuit sculptures and other crafts complete this excellent collection.

HIGHLIGHTS

- Emily Carr's *Corner of Kitwancool Village*
- Lawren Harris's *Mt Lefroy*
- J. E. H. MacDonald's *Forest Wilderness*
- A. Y. Jackson's *First Snow*
- Tom Thomson's *Wood Interior, Winter*
- Arthur Lismer's *Bright Land*
- F. H. Varley's *Night Ferry*
- First Nations art
- Inuit sculpture

INFORMATION

- Off map to northwest; Locator map A1
- Islington Avenue, Kleinburg
- 905/893-1121; www.mcmichael.com
- Mon–Fri 10–4, Sat 11–4, Sun 11–5, May–Oct; Tue–Fri 10–4, Sat–Sun 11–4, rest of year
- Restaurant, cafeteria
- Good
- Moderate
- Paramount Canada's Wonderland (➤ 28)
- Weekend tours at 1pm; special events

Above: A. Y. Jackson, The Red Maple (1914) detail

27

Paramount Canada's Wonderland

INFORMATION

🚩 Off map to northwest; Locator map A1

✉ 9580 Jane Street Vaughan. Take Hwy 400 to Rutherford Road

☎ 905/832-7000; www.canadas-wonderland.com

🕐 Daily 10–6, May; 10–8, early Jun; 9–10, mid-Jun to Labour Day; Sat, Sun 10–8, Sep–2nd week in Oct

🍴 Many outlets

🚇 Yorkdale or York Mills and then GO bus

♿ Few

💲 Expensive (One Price Passport). Additional fees for karts, theater, mini-golf, Xtreme Skyflyer

🔁 McMichael Collection (► 27), Black Creek Pioneer Village (► 29)

❓ Special events from fireworks to video dance fests

Rollercoaster riders revel in this park, for it contains 12 coasters—enough to satisfy even the most jaded addict. The park has more than 65 rides and 200 attractions—adding new thrillers every year to keep the locals coming back.

Gut-wrenchers Shockwave spins and loops riders through 360° and 70ft (21m) into the air with immense force. Another thriller is the daredevil Drop Zone, which takes riders 230ft (70m) up and then drops them, in an open carriage, in a 60mph (96kph) free fall. A further heart-stopping experience awaits you at the Xtreme Skyflyer, which elevates you to 150ft (45m) and then delivers the combined thrills of skydiving and hang-gliding. Still, the rollercoasters remain the perennial favorites: the looping inverted Top Gun, a standing loop version called Sky Rider, a wooden coaster for nostalgia seekers, and several other metal coasters.

Water plus Splashworks, the 20-acre (8-ha) water park, is another major attraction. It contains an extra-large wave pool generating white caps, and 18 different water slides, including one with eight stories and another involving a 400-ft (120-m) drop in the dark. There's also a wacky aquatic jungle gym for small children.

Less strenuous If you tire of flipping your stomach, then there are plenty of other things to do: the Kingswood Theatre, where musical groups entertain; encounters with ferocious monsters in a 3-D movie ride at the Paramount Action F/X Theatre; street entertainment by Hanna-Barbera characters and Nickleodeon's Rugrats in Kidzville; and batting cages and mini golf. At Speed City Raceway, there are two-seater karts.

Black Creek Pioneer Village

This living history park re-creates 19th-century Ontario village life as authentically as possible. Leave behind the stresses of modern times and step back into the past to find out about existence in a pioneer community.

Family farm Black Creek is built around the Stong family farm—their first log house (1816), smokehouse and barn (1825), and a second clapboard home that they built in 1832. Even the sheep and hogs are authentic, since they are imported English breeds that would have been familiar to the 19th-century pioneers.

Village life The village consists of some 30 mid-19th-century buildings. Wandering along the pathways and boardwalks between them, you seem to slip into a slower pace of life, one established by the horse rather than the automobile. Seeds are sold at the Laskay Emporium store, along with old-fashioned candy and handcrafted brooms made in the village. Half Way House, so called because it stood halfway between York and Scarborough, is a stagecoach tavern. Every day loaves are baked here in the old hearth oven. These convincing surroundings are brought to life by the artisans who take delight in passing on their skills and knowledge. The cooper hunches over the barrel stove compressing staves to make watertight barrels and pails held together without a single nail. Others demonstrate tinsmithing, weaving, cabinetmaking, blacksmithing, clockmaking and printing. Dickson's Hill School is a one-room schoolhouse that nevertheless has separate entrances for boys and girls. The gardens include a herb garden with 42 familiar herbs, the weaver's dye garden containing plants like bloodroot (red), sunflowers (yellow) and woad (blue), and the doctor's medicinal garden.

HIGHLIGHTS

- Coopering
- Tinsmithing
- Flour milling
- Pioneer gardens
- Laskay Emporium and post office
- Half Way House

INFORMATION

- ✛ Off map to north; Locator map A1
- ✉ 1000 Murray Ross Parkway, North York
- ☎ 416/736-1733; www.blackcreek.ca
- 🕐 Mon–Fri 9.30–4.30, Sat–Sun 10–5, May–Jun; daily 10–5, Jul–Sep; Mon–Fri 9.30–4, Sat–Sun 10–4.30, Oct–Dec
- 🍴 Restaurant, coffee cart
- 🚇 Jane subway and 35B bus; Finch subway and 60E bus
- ♿ Few
- 💵 Moderate
- ↔ Paramount Canada's Wonderland (▶ 28)

Ontario Place

INFORMATION

✚ F10; Locator map A4

✉ 955 Lake Shore Boulevard West, between Dufferin and Strachan Avenue

☎ 416/314-9811 or 416/314-9900; www.ontarioplace.com

🕐 Daily 10.30–midnight, mid-May to Labour Day. Most attractions close at dusk

🍴 Many restaurants and snack bars

🚋 Streetcar 509 from Union Station, or streetcar 511 Bathurst–Exhibition Place

♿ Good

💲 Expensive

↔ Fort York (➤ 31)

❓ Special events, including fireworks

This weird and wonderful waterfront recreation complex, a futuristic-looking creation of the 1970s, boasts rides, activities and attractions aimed at visitors of all ages.

Always up-to-date Ontario Place is spread over three artificial islands and adds up to a 96-acre (38-ha) park with rides, attractions, top-name performers, IMAX films, stage shows and restaurants. The original Ontario Place, designed in 1971 by architects Craig-Zeidler-Strong of Toronto, won many awards for excellence. To keep it up to date, new attractions are added every year.

Water, water everywhere At Children's Village, an imaginative play park, youngsters can scramble over rope bridges, bounce on a trampoline, squirt water pistols at each other and enjoy the entertainment on the Festival Stage. The two waterslides, the Pink Twister and the Purple Pipeline, are not far behind in popularity and neither is the flume called Wilderness Adventure Ride. For daredevils there is the Hydrofuge, a tubular waterslide that sends riders speeding at 30mph (50kph) into a spinning bowl before depositing them into a 6ft- (2m-) deep pool. Sea Trek is a deep-sea submarine simulator; or you can shoot the rapids on the Rush River attraction.

Entertainment too Other attractions are inside eye-catching steel and glass structures—"pods." The Lego Pod has huge Lego creations, while the Thrill Zone Pod features many simulator experiences and video games. The Molson Amphitheatre seats 16,000 (including 7,000 on the lawns) for stellar summer performances. The Atlantis Complex contains several restaurants and lounges and features an evening dance club.

Fort York

This complex of buildings sandwiched between the railroad tracks and the highway will give you a historic jolt back to 1813 when muddy York was a rough-and-ready imperial outpost.

Fort York and the White House On 27 April, 1813, during the War of 1812, 2,700 Americans stormed ashore from Lake Ontario. They drove out the troops at Fort York and set fire to Government House and the Parliament Buildings. In 1814, in retaliation, the British occupied Washington and burned the president's residence. According to Canadian legend, the Americans covered up the blackened walls with white paint, and from then on it was called the White House, but the Americans say it was named for the color of the stone.

Military memorabilia John Graves Simcoe built a garrison on the site of Fort York in 1793. The fort was strengthened in 1811 (the west wall and circular battery date from that time) and, shortly after the events of 1813, the British rebuilt it; most of the fort's buildings date from then. The officers' quarters (1815) have been meticulously furnished to reflect the late 1830s. The Blue Barracks has exhibits on Canadian military history from the War of 1812 to the trench warfare of World War I. In Blockhouse 2, which served as 160-man barracks, a video and dioramas relate the history of the fort. The East Magazine (1814) displays some of the 12,000 artifacts retrieved, documenting the officers' daily life—buckles, heel plates, buttons, baleen tweezers. The Stone Magazine (1815) provided bombproof storage for 900 barrels of gunpowder within its 6ft- (2m-) thick walls.

HIGHLIGHTS

* Officers' Quarters
* Stone Magazine

INFORMATION

* G9; Locator map C4
* Garrison Road, off Fleet Street between Bathurst Street and Strachan Avenue
* 416/392-6907; www.toronto.ca/culture
* Daily 10–5, Victoria Day–Labour Day; Mon–Fri 10–4; Sat–Sun 10–5, rest of year
* Bathurst 511 streetcar
* Few
* Inexpensive
* SkyDome (➤ 36), CN Tower (➤ 37), The Pier (➤ 56)
* Tours by interpreters in period costume. Jul–Aug: drills, musket and cannon firing, fife and drum music

Casa Loma

HIGHLIGHTS

- Great Hall
- Oak Room
- Conservatory

INFORMATION

- ✚ H5; Locator map C1
- ✉ 1 Austin Terrace at Davenport and Spadina Road
- ☎ 416/923-1171; www.casaloma.org
- ⏰ House daily 9.30–5; gardens 9.30–5, May–Oct
- 🍴 Café
- Ⓓ Dupont
- ♿ Good
- 💵 Moderate
- ❓ Self-guided tour; garden talks

The Great Hall at Casa Loma

A mixture of 17th-century Scottish baronial and 20th Century Fox, Casa Loma is a rich man's folly. It cost $3.5 million to build, yet after real estate changes, only ten years later was valued at an astonishing $27,305.

Splendor Canadian-style A magnificent and whimsical place with its Elizabethan chimneys, Rhenish turrets, underground tunnels and secret passageways, Casa Loma is Sir Henry Pellatt's fantasy of what constituted European aristocratic splendor. Between 1911 and 1914 Pellatt created this fantasy home, importing Scottish stonemasons and Italian woodcarvers to embellish it, then spending an additional $1.5 million furnishing the 98 rooms. The results are grand. A hammerbeam ceiling covers the 66ft- (20m-) high Great Hall; three artisans took three years to carve the paneling in the Oak Room; splendid bronze doors lead into the marble conservatory crowned with a stained-glass dome. Modern conveniences and luxuries included an elevator, a private telephone system, marble swimming pool, 10,000-volume library, 15 baths and 5,000 electric lights. One underground tunnel runs out to the stables, where the horses, stabled amid the luxury of Spanish tile and mahogany, had their names set in 18-carat gold letters at the head of each stall.

The bubble bursts The son of a stockbroker, Pellatt went into the brokerage business after college, and bought huge blocks of stock in the Northwest Land Company and the Canadian Pacific Railway. By 1910 he had amassed $17 million. Still in his 20s, he founded Toronto's first hydroelectric power company, but his wealth evaporated in 1920 when electric power was ruled a public utility. Pellatt was eventually to decline into poverty, and died penniless in 1939.

Kensington Market

Throughout its history, Kensington Market has been the domain of the major immigrant group of the decade. Once Jewish, then Portuguese, today it is more Asian/Caribbean than anything else. Saturday is the busiest day.

Multiethnic tastes There is no central market square, just a series of narrow streets—notably Kensington and Augusta Avenues, and Baldwin Street—lined with stores selling all kinds of provisions. On Kensington Avenue there are several West Indian grocery stores selling yucca, sugarcane, plantains, papaya, mangoes and other tropical items. Don't miss Mendel's Creamery, with such delights as smoked fish, herring, cheeses and gigantic dill pickles. Global Cheese, next door, offers an around-the-world education in cheeses. Portuguese fish markets, like Medeiro's, line much of Baldwin Street. Outside each storefront, boxes are piled high with flat, stiff dried cod.

Snacking Wonderful aromas waft out of the Baldwin Street Bakery, which is worth a stop for a croissant. Other stores on Baldwin display all kinds of grains, beans, nuts and fruits. Pick up an energizing snack of dried papaya, mango, pineapple or apricots at Salamanca, along with some pecans or filberts from Casa Acoreana. Around the corner, on Augusta Avenue, go into Perola Supermarket to see the cassava and the myriad varieties of peppers and medicinal roots that are for sale here. In the back of the store you'll find a woman selling tasty *pupusas*, which are meat- and cheese-filled *tamales*. In Dennison Square enjoy a quiet moment seated on the bronze benches at the life-size statue dedicated to Canada's most beloved actor "the King" (➤ 11, panel).

HIGHLIGHTS

- Mendel's Creamery
- Global Cheese
- Medeiro's Fish Market
- Baldwin Street Bakery
- Salamanca
- Casa Acoreana
- Perola Supermarket

INFORMATION

- H7; Locator map C3
- Bounded by Spadina and Augusta Avenues between College and St. Andrews
- Stores open normal hours
- Dundas or College streetcar
- Chinatown (➤ 52)

Bata Shoe Museum

INFORMATION

- ✚ H6; Locator map D2
- ✉ 327 Bloor Street
- ☎ 416/979-7799; www. batashoemuseum.ca
- 🕐 Tue–Wed, Fri–Sat 10–5, Thu 10–8, Sun noon–5
- Ⓢ St. George
- ♿ Excellent
- 💵 Moderate
- ↔ University of Toronto (➤ 35), ROM (➤ 40), George R. Gardiner Museum (➤ 41), Yorkville (➤ 53)
- ❓ Lectures, workshops, storytelling programs

Imelda Marcos would be in her element at this museum. Housed in a structure resembling a shoe box, there are over 10,000 items in the displays of footwear past and present.

More than just shoes The main permanent exhibit traces the history of shoes from the first footprint made 3.7 million years ago in Tanzania to the extraordinary shoes of today. The sheer variety of beautiful and truly striking footwear is amazing. Each display is set against an appropriate series of cutouts reflecting the particular period or geographic location. There are all kinds of ceremonial shoes: leather sandals with gilded images worn by the King of Kumasi in Ghana for state occasions; wedding shoes from various cultures; and lacquered and painted shoes worn to Shinto shrines in Japan. The museum is a goldmine of little-known facts; for instance, that Elizabeth I was in part responsible for the foot problems caused by high heels because it was she who popularized them in an attempt to make herself appear taller. The style was limited to the elite, hence the term "well-heeled." Toe-length was another important indicator of social status; in England, in the mid-14th century, anyone earning under 40 livres was not allowed to wear pointed toes, a nobleman could wear shoes with toes 24in (69cm) long, and a prince could wear shoes with toes of any length. The display culminates in "The Shoes of the Stars"—Picasso's mock zebra lace-ups, Elton John's 12-in (30-cm) high platform shoes, and the sandals worn by former Canadian premier Pierre Trudeau when he was hiking around the world.

Right: Elton John's platforms

University of Toronto

Important scientific discoveries have been made at this venerable institution, most notably insulin. It also numbers many world-famous names among its past students and teachers.

Famous alumni and remarkable research Founded in 1827, this is Canada's largest university with more than 50,000 students. The university's scientific achievements include pioneering work that led to the development of the laser; the first electronic heart pacemaker; and the discovery of the gene responsible for the most severe form of Alzheimer's Disease. Notable alumni include authors Margaret Atwood, Farley Mowat and Stephen Leacock; figures from the movie world Atom Egoyan, Norman Jewison and Donald Sutherland; opera singers Teresa Stratas and Maureen Forrester; and prime ministers Mackenzie King and Lester Pearson.

Gothic and modern Stroll around the downtown main St. George campus to view the mixture of architecture. On Hoskin Avenue see Wycliffe and Trinity Colleges, the first a monument of redbrick Romanesque Revival and the second a Gothic complex with chapel and eye-catching gardens. Around the corner on Devonshire Place, Massey College is a 1960s building; writer Robertson Davies was Master here for many years. The heart of the university is Hart House, consciously modeled on Magdalen College, Oxford, with its impressive Gallery Grill. See the collection of Canadian art in the Justina M. Barnicke Art Gallery in the west wing. Just south of Hart House is the Romanesque revival University College, with an arts center (► 56, panel) in the Laidlaw Building. King's College Circle passes by several other stately university buildings.

DID YOU KNOW?

- Engineering pioneer Ursula Franklin is a professor emeritus
- Immunologist and virologist Dr. Tak Mak, the first to clone a T-cell gene, is on the faculty
- The university's Dr. Lap Chee Tsui was on the team that discovered the cystic fibrosis gene
- The Royal Ontario Museum, the Canadian Opera Company and the Toronto Symphony all started here
- Hypersonic flight (Mach 5) was pioneered here with the first airplane powered by microwaves

INFORMATION

- ✚ J6, J7; Locator map D2
- ✉ West of Queen's Park
- ☎ 416/978-5000; www.utoronto.ca
- 🍴 Gallery Grill in Hart House and numerous cafeterias in campus buildings
- Ⓜ Museum or Queen's Park
- ⬛ College Street streetcar
- ♿ Good
- 🎟 Free
- ↔ ROM (► 40), George R. Gardiner Museum (► 41), Ontario Legislature (► 42)
- ❓ Tours year round. Special tours Jun–Aug

35

SkyDome

The home of the Blue Jays in downtown Toronto is so revolutionary in design that it has become an attraction with an organized tour. In the stadium hotel you can even rent a suite with a grandstand view of the field.

HIGHLIGHTS

- Retractable roof
- Video explaining the stadium's construction
- Corporate skyboxes
- Press facilities
- Dressing room
- Hotel overlooking the field

The Audience (1988–89) by Michael Snow (► 59, panel)

INFORMATION

- H9–J9; Locator map D4
- 1 Blue Jays Way
- 416/341-2770; www.skydome.com. For Blue Jays game tickets 416/341-1234 well ahead
- Restaurants, cafés and snackbars
- Union Station
- Front Street streetcars
- Very good
- Moderate
- CN Tower (► 37)
- Tours

Engineering feat Numbers help to illustrate the great engineering feat represented by the stadium. One of the largest in Major League baseball ever built, it has a fully retractable roof and required much engineering ingenuity in its design and execution. The 11,000-tonne roof covers nearly 8 acres (3ha) and there are 250,000 roof bolts, yet it can be opened in 20 minutes thanks to the ingenious steel track and the trucks driven by 10-horsepower motors. Although the tour film is cloying beyond belief, it does offer a glimpse of what it was like to build this vast structure. When the camera pans up the girders, their height is truly scary.

Tour topics On the tour, visitors are given a mass of statistics about the astroturf, and how long it takes for it all to be stuck together; you visit one of the astronomically expensive corporate skyboxes and take a look at the broadcast/press facilities. The stadium incorporates an 11-story hotel where the rooms have great views facing onto the field and can be rented on game nights for upward of $800. The Toronto Blue Jays Clubhouse is off limits to visitors, except occasionally during the March break, but you can have a peek (when events permit) at the visiting team's dressing room. The Toronto Argonauts (Canadian Football League) also play here; other entertainment ranges from circuses to pop concerts and ice shows.

CN Tower

The CN Tower is Toronto's trademark. Like San Francisco's TransAmerica and Seattle's Space Needle, it was derided at first but ultimately embraced by citizens. At 1,815ft (553m), it is the world's tallest free-standing tower.

On a clear day It's certainly a stomach-churning experience to rocket at 20ft (6m) per second in glass-fronted elevators to the SkyPod's observation deck. On arrival, you step out onto a glass floor and peer down at the ground, 1,135ft (346m) below. From the outdoor observation deck, on a clear day, you can see the mist of Niagara Falls on the other side of the lake. You can also take the elevator another 33 stories up to the SkyPod at 1,463ft (446m). The tower has attracted record-seekers—including Ashrita Furman, who bounced on his pogo stick up the 1,967 steps to the SkyPod roof in 57 minutes and 43 seconds.

Shopping and other entertainments Down at the base of the tower there's hands-on action in the Edge Arcade, featuring simulated game experiences like Indy Racing and Alpine Racer. The Ultimate Roller Coaster takes you on a pitch-and-roll ride, while the Easy Glide Canadian Panorama is a more sedate trip though the Rockies. The Maple Leaf Theatre shows a 22-minute film "Momentum-Images" of Canada. The Marketplace offers varied shopping. Before you go up the tower, check out the touch-screen kiosks that tell the story of how it was built. Here too, let the daredevil in you imagine the thrill of bungee jumping from the observation level or walking on a tightrope to neighboring skyscrapers.

HIGHLIGHTS

- Glass floor
- View from observation deck
- SkyPod
- Edge Arcade
- Maple Leaf Theatre
- Simulator rides
- The ride up

INFORMATION

- J9; Locator map D4
- 301 Front Street West
- 416/360-8500; www.cntower.ca
- Tower daily 8am–11pm (9–11 in winter). Other attractions vary
- 360 Restaurant 416/362-5411, Horizons, Marketplace Café
- Union Station
- Front Street streetcar
- Very good
- Observation deck expensive; games expensive
- SkyDome (➤ 36)

Art Gallery of Ontario

INFORMATION

- J8; Locator map D3
- 317 Dundas Street West
- 416/979-6648; www.ago.net
- Tue, Thu–Fri 11–6, Wed 11–8.30, Sat–Sun 10–5.30
- Agora Restaurant
- St. Patrick
- Dundas streetcar
- Very good
- Moderate
- Chinatown (► 52), Museum for Textiles (► 56), Eaton Centre (► 72)
- Tours, lectures, films, concerts

Boldly painted to great effect, this is a showcase for Canadian and European art. There is also a superb collection of sculptures by Henry Moore. The whole gallery is arranged around the historic Grange (► 39).

Canada's best The Canadian artists known as the Group of Seven (► 27) had their first show here in 1920, and the galleries displaying their works are exceptional. See Tom Thomson's *The West Wind* (1917), J. E. H. MacDonald's *Falls, Montreal River* (1920), Lawren Harris's *Above Lake Superior* (1922) and Emily Carr's *Indian Church* (1929). Other galleries trace the development of Canadian art. Look for Joseph Legare's *The Fire in the Saint Jean Quarter Seen Looking Westward* (1845), James Wilson Morrice's *Gibraltar* (1913), Paul Emile Borduas' *Woman with Jewel* (1945), Paterson Ewen's *Coastal Trip* (1974), Joanne Tod's *Similac* (1992) and Jeff Wall's *The Goat* (1989). Don't miss the Inuit galleries, with sculptures, prints and drawings.

Henry Moore collection The Henry Moore Sculpture Centre, which opened in 1974, houses one of the largest public collections of his works. A series of color photographs shows many of Moore's major works in their original locations.

From the Old World Of European art, most noteworthy are the 17th-century works by Luca Giordano, Antoine Coypel, Jean-Baptiste Jouvenet and Jusepe de Ribera, as well as some fine Florentine baroque bronzes. The gallery has works by Picasso, Dufy, Modigliani, Brancusi, Gauguin, Chagall, Barbara Hepworth, Naum Gabo and the surrealists. There are also collections of photographs, prints and drawings, and an outstanding film archive.

The Grange

This house museum gives an insight into an era when the city was a much less liberal place, ruled by a handful of powermongers, referred to collectively as the Family Compact. It offers a fascinating glimpse of how one family lived.

The Boulton family home   When Harriette Dixon Boulton Smith died in 1909, she bequeathed the Grange and its 6 acres (2.5ha) of parkland to the then homeless Art Gallery of Ontario (► 38). It was originally the home of D'Arcy Boulton, Jr. who built it in 1817 on 100 acres (40ha). The Boultons were members of the ruling elite and the house became a center of social and political life. D'Arcy occupied a series of government positions and his son, William Henry, was Mayor of Toronto four times. When William Henry died, his widow married Goldwin Smith, journalist and professor of modern history at Oxford, who entertained lavishly. Among the visitors were Edward, the Prince of Wales, and Winston Churchill.

Upper-class Toronto in 1840   The house is decorated to represent life as it was in the mid-19th century and the contents of each room are described on paddleboards. Downstairs, the pier table in the dining room provoked criticism of the family because it was made in the United States, while the pole fire screen in the parlor guarded fashionably pallid complexions against a rosy glow. Upstairs there are two bedrooms and a large music room, where parties and balls were held. The most interesting part of the residence is the servants' quarters. Down here a fire burns in the hearth adjacent to the bake oven. Here, too, are some historical exhibits documenting the wealth of most of the other members of the Family Compact.

HIGHLIGHTS

- Dining room
- Bedrooms
- Breakfast parlor
- Music room
- Kitchen
- Fire in the hearth
- Whatever has come out of the oven on the day

INFORMATION

- ✚ J8; Locator map D3
- ✉ 317 Dundas Street West
- ☎ 416/977-0414; www.ago.net
- 🕐 Tue, Thu–Sun noon–4, Wed noon–8.30
- 🍴 Restaurant at Art Gallery of Ontario
- 🚇 St. Patrick
- 🚋 Dundas streetcar
- ♿ Few
- 💲 Moderate
- ↔ Art Gallery of Ontario (► 38), Chinatown (► 52), Eaton Centre (► 72)
- ❓ Self-guided tours

Above: The Grange's enormous kitchen

Royal Ontario Museum

HIGHLIGHTS

- Bishop White Gallery
- The Ming tomb
- Life Sciences Galleries
- Birdsong computer terminals
- Bat cave
- Gem and gold room

INFORMATION

- J6; Locator map D2
- 100 Queen's Park
- 416/586-5549 or 416/586-8000; www.rom.on.ca
- Mon–Thu, Sat 10–6, Fri 10–9.30, Sun 11–6
- JK ROM (➤ 63, panel, lunch only), Druxey's
- Museum
- Excellent
- Expensive
- Bata Shoe Museum (➤ 34), George R. Gardiner Museum (➤ 41), Yorkville (➤ 53)

Among the 40 galleries and 6 million objects at the museum, you'll find dinosaurs, an eerie bat cave, one of the world's foremost Chinese collections and a remarkable collection of European and Canadian decorative arts.

East and west The T. T. Tsui Chinese galleries display bones used as oracles, bronze vessels, Han jades and T'ang dynasty earthenware warriors. A Ming tomb is accompanied by a model of a Chinese house (buried in the tomb), while the Levy Court contains traditional room settings from the Ming and Qing dynasties plus a lovely collection of snuff bottles and a fine ceramics gallery. Particularly impressive are the wall paintings and monumental sculptures (12th–16th centuries) in the Bishop White Gallery of Chinese Temple Art. Mummies are the favorites in the Egyptian galleries; pottery, jewelry, sculpture, coins and glassware fill the Greek and Roman galleries. The Samuel European Galleries exhibit arms and armor, and some exquisite period rooms. The Sigmund Samuel Canadiana gallery showcases Canadian decorative arts. The gallery of Korean art opened in 1999.

A buddha from the T. T. Tsui Chinese Galleries

The natural world The Life Sciences Galleries on evolution, insects, mammals and birds are well conceived. The bird galleries, for instance, include a realistic diorama of the Ontario wetlands, and invite visitors to explore birdsong at several computer terminals. The bat cave is a replica of the St. Clair Cave in Jamaica. The dinosaur galleries contain 13 realistically displayed skeletons. In the gem and gold room don't miss the 2,998-carat blue topaz.

George R. Gardiner Museum

This outstanding display of fine pottery and porcelain, highlighting particular historical periods, was amassed by collectors George and Helen Gardiner. Though small, the museum is diverse enough to provide plenty of interest.

Colorful earthenware On the ground level is a marvelous collection of pre-Columbian pottery. The figures and vessels date from 3000BC to the 16th century and range from Mexico to Peru. Among them are some remarkable pieces by the Olmecs, red clay Nayarit figures, Zacatecan-style male statuettes with mushroom-shaped horns, extraordinary smiling figures from Nopiloa, Los Cerros, or Isla de Sacrificios, fine orange and plumbate ware of the Mayans and Aztec objects. The next great period of ceramic art is represented by colorful Italian majolica from the 15th and 16th centuries, and there is a selection of English tin-glazed earthenware, including the familiar blue and white Delftware.

Delicate porcelain The next floor is devoted entirely to porcelain, including figures by Meissen's famous sculptor-potter Joachim Kändler and some prime examples of Sèvres. English porcelain is well represented, from the early softpaste pieces manufactured at Chelsea and Bow to the later bone china that was invented by Josiah Spode. The collection also features 120 figures from the *commedia dell'arte* and 100 mid-18th-century scent bottles, with examples ranging from early Meissen to highly decorated rococo versions from various sources.

HIGHLIGHTS

- Olmec figures
- Smiling figures
- Majolica
- *Commedia dell'arte* figures
- Scent bottles

INFORMATION

- J6; Locator map E2
- 111 Queen's Park
- 416/586-8080; www.gardinermuseum.on.ca
- Mon, Wed, Fri 10–6, Tue, Thu 10–8, Sat, Sun 10–5
- Museum
- Very good
- Free (donation requested)
- Bata Shoe Museum (➤ 34), University of Toronto (➤ 35), Royal Ontario Museum (➤ 40), Ontario Legislature (➤ 42), Yorkville (➤ 53)
- Tours, lectures

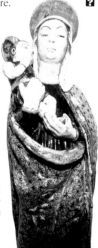

Above: Meso-American exhibits
Right: Majolica Madonna and Child

41

Ontario Legislature

INFORMATION

- J7; Locator map E2
- Queen's Park
- 416/325-7500; www.ontla.on.ca
- Sessions Mar–Jun and Sep–Dec
- Cafeteria
- Queen's Park
- Good
- Free
- Bata Shoe Museum (➤ 34), University of Toronto (➤ 35), Royal Ontario Museum (➤ 40), George R. Gardiner Museum (➤ 41)
- Tours: daily Victoria Day–Labor Day; weekdays only Sep–May. Reservations needed

Most parliamentary institutions deliver great free entertainment, and the Ontario Provincial legislature is no exception, with the 130 members heckling, jeering and cheering each other as they debate and pass laws.

Parliamentary session In this impressive four-story chamber the laws affecting 9 million Ontarians are passed. On a dais sits the Speaker who presides over the house. To the right sits the Government, to the left, the Opposition. In the center is the Clerks' table with the mace. Behind the Clerks' table is a smaller table for Hansard record-keepers. On the steps of the dais sit the Legislative Pages who run errands in the house. Above the Speaker is the press gallery. Parliamentary sessions are opened and closed by the Lieutenant Governor representing Queen Elizabeth II. The highlight of any day in the chamber is the question time period when members bombard the premier and cabinet ministers with questions.

Architectural and historical grandeur Even if the house is not sitting you can tour the building, a massive Romanesque revival structure made out of reddish-brown sandstone, opened in 1893. A grand staircase lined with portraits of Ontario premiers sweeps up to the chamber above. An enormous stained-glass ceiling-window lights the East Wing where the premier has his office. The west lobby has mosaic floors, and Italian marble columns in the beaux-arts style, with elaborately carved capitals. On the ground level are historical and regional exhibits, including the original provincial mace which was stolen by the Americans during the 1812 war and only returned under Franklin D. Roosevelt in 1934.

Harbourfront

This development is a wonderful example of a waterfront park that is not just a glorified shopping mall. It's a place to spend the whole day—biking, sailing, canoeing, picnicking, watching craftspeople and even shopping.

Lakefront leisure Start at Queen's Quay where, in an old warehouse building, there is an attractive shopping mall with specialty shops. Several restaurants have outside dining areas from which to enjoy the waterfront. Take the lakeside walking trail to York Quay, stopping en route at the Power Plant, a contemporary art gallery, and the Du Maurier Theatre Centre behind it. On York Quay you'll find artisans glassmaking, pot-throwing, jewelry making, silk-screening or metal sculpting. You can purchase the results in the adjacent store. York Quay's lakefront has a small pond, a children's play area and the outdoor Harbourfront Centre Concert Stage. Across the footbridge is John Quay with several restaurants, while the next quay has boats to rent (► below).

The place to rent a boat In good weather, Harbourfront is a good place to relax on the grass or people-watch from one of the waterfront cafés. Alternatively, sail- and power-boats can be rented or you can sign up for sailing lessons at the Harbourside Boating Centre ☎ 416/203-3000. Harbourfront holds more than 4,000 events of all sorts, from the Milk International Children's Festival (► 59, panel) to the International Festival of Authors in October or the First Night Celebration of the Arts in December.

HIGHLIGHTS

● Shopping at Queen's Quay
● Art exhibits at the Power Plant
● Craft Studio

INFORMATION

✚ J9; Locator map E4
✉ Harbourfront Centre, 235 Queen's Quay West
☎ 416/973-3000
🕔 York Quay Centre daily 11–9. Queen's Quay Mon–Sat 10–9, Sun 10–6
🍴 Several
🚊 510 streetcar from Union

Queen's Quay terminal

♿ Very good
💲 Free
↔ SkyDome (► 36), CN Tower (► 37)
❓ Many special events (information at York Quay)

43

City Hall

INFORMATION

- J8; Locator map E3
- Queen Street West
- 416/338-0338; www.toronto.ca
- Cafeteria
- Queen or Osgoode
- Very good
- Free
- Campbell House (➤ 55), Osgoode Hall (➤ 55)
- Self-guided tour

Remarkable for its striking design, which shook up Toronto in the early 1960s, City Hall could be a space station, with the council chamber a flying saucer cradled between two semicircular control towers.

Viljo Revell and Nathan Phillips When Mayor Nathan Phillips persuaded the City Council to hold a competition to design a new city hall, the councillors found themselves looking at 520 submissions from 42 countries. Finnish architect Viljo Revell was announced the winner, and his building opened in 1965. The square in front serves as a site for community entertainment; the reflecting pool, where workers eat sandwiches in summer, turns into a skating rink in winter. To the east of City Hall the peace garden contains an eternal flame lit by Pope John Paul II using a flame from the Memorial for Peace at Hiroshima. Near the entrance stands Henry Moore's *Three Way Piece Number Two*, affectionately called *The Archer* by Torontonians.

Open government and municipal art City Hall itself contains several art works. Just inside the entrance, the mural *Metropolis*, by local artist David Partridge, is created from more than 100,000 nails. Continue into the Rotunda and the Hall of Memory, shaped like a sunken amphitheater, where, in the Golden Book, are listed 3,500 Torontonians who died in World War II. At its center rises a large white column supporting the Council Chamber above. The north corridor is lined with a copper and glass mosaic called *Views to the City*, depicting historic panoramic views of the city skyline. From here you can take an elevator up to the Council Chamber, which is open to the public unless there's a private meeting.

The Hockey Hall of Fame

There's a Canadian saying: first you walk, then you skate. Hockey is to Canadians what football is to the Americans. It's the one game that most Canadians want to watch and take part in.

The Stanley Cup and Hall of Fame The jewel of the museum is the Bell Great Hall, once the grand banking hall of the Bank of Montreal. Here the Stanley Cup, North America's oldest professional sports trophy, is displayed in front of the Honoured Members Wall.

Live action At the Rink Zone you will find live shooting booths with sticks and a pail full of pucks; or you can test your goal-keeping skills in front of a TV monitor. At the Impact Zone (for a small charge) you can pad up and play at rookie, professional or all-star level against Wayne Gretzky and Mark Messier, who fire sponge pucks at full speed from a video screen.

Eavesdrop In an exact replica of the hallowed dressing room of the Montreal Canadiens, you can spy on the player routines before the game and listen to Dick Irvin Senior and Junior compare today's sports medicine—laser therapy, ultrasound and electro massage—with the rub and bandage approach of yesterday. There are memorabilia of teams and players, movie clips of great moments and displays on the evolution of equipment, from early sticks, like tree branches, to modern aluminum versions and from early leather masks to the personalized ones (shark teeth, panther jaws) preferred by goalies today.

HIGHLIGHTS

- Stanley Cup
- Rink Zone
- Montreal Canadiens' dressing room
- Impact Zone
- Great Moments Video

INFORMATION

- K9; Locator map E3
- BCE Place at Front and Yonge
- 416/360-7765; www.hhof.com
- Mon–Sat 9.30–6, Sun 10–6, Jun–Aug; Mon–Fri 10–5, Sat 9.30–6, Sun 10.30–5, rest of year
- King and Union
- King Street streetcar
- Very good
- Expensive
- St. Lawrence Market (➤ 47)

Above: The Stanley Cup
Below: Hockey sculpture

45

The Toronto Islands

HIGHLIGHTS

- Centreville
- Hanlan's Point
- View from Algonquin Island

INFORMATION

- Off map south of harbor. Ferries J9–K9; Locator map B2
- Centreville 416/203-0405. Ferry 416/392-8193

A mere 20-minute ferry ride takes you to this peaceful archipelago of meandering waterways, cycle paths and bucolic lanes, which seems light years away from the bustling city you left behind.

A city retreat Originally a peninsula, shattered by a storm in 1858, the 14 Toronto islands incorporate 600 acres (243ha), crisscrossed by shady paths and laced with quiet waterways and inlets. Until around 1920 there were grand hotels here. Today people come to walk, bike, play tennis, feed the ducks, picnic, sit on the beach or go boating. There are public swimming areas on Centre and Ward's Island (and a "clothing optional"—nude—beach at Hanlan's Point, only the second one in Canada) but they are often polluted and signposted as such.

Centre, Ward's and Algonquin These are the main islands. The first is the busiest, with Centreville—an old-fashioned amusement park with an 1890s carousel, a flume ride, antique cars and a small working farm where children can pet the lambs and ride the ponies. From Centre Island you can take a 45-minute walk to either Hanlan's Point or Ward's Island and catch a return ferry. The other two islands support a community of some 600 residents who live a simple life. On Ward's Island you can walk along the boardwalk to a bridge across the lagoon to Algonquin Island, where there is a spectacular view of the city skyline. The best way to explore is to rent a bike when you get off the ferry and ride from one end of the island to the other, or to take the free tram from Centre Island out to Hanlan's Point.

Fun on Centreville

- Several restaurants/cafés
- Harbourfront LRT or Bay 6 and Spadina 77B buses
- Centreville ferry service operates aproximately every 45 minutes in winter but the service is more frequent in summer
- Few
- Ferry Inexpensive
- Seasonal events

St. Lawrence Market

The lofty 19th-century building that houses this market is entirely worthy of the rich and colorful displays within. This is the place to taste a Canadian peameal bacon sandwich or amass the ingredients for a picnic banquet.

Food lovers' favorites Among the many stalls are a few favorites. At Sausage King you'll find ten or more types of salami—Hungarian, bierwurst, Black Forest wurst and more. Combine any one with the breads at the Carousel Bakery—sourdough, focaccia, Portuguese cornbread or pani Calabrese—or grab a peameal bacon sandwich for breakfast (the flavor of the bacon is deliciously enriched by its coating of ground dried peas). Go to Mano's Deli for pastrami or corned beef or Debrezeni sausages on a bun with plenty of kraut, relish and mustard. Great wheels of cheese can be found at Alex's Farm, from Stilton to Camembert. Any picnic will be enhanced by the chocolate butter tarts, skor brownies or other pastries sold at Future Bakery. And for good measure, why not throw in some Quebec terrines (rabbit and pistachio, wild boar and apricot, pheasant and mushroom) or pâtés (goose liver, venison), or shrimp and lobster mousse from Scheffler's Deli. Downstairs in the market you'll find Caviar Direct, as well as other stalls offering a variety of foods, including 33 different kinds of rice at Rube's.

Fresh from the fields This old market is a treat any day, but Saturday is perhaps the best day to come, because that is when the farmers set up stalls at daybreak in the Farmers' Market building across the street, selling fresh produce, preserves, fresh baking, meat, and arts and crafts.

HIGHLIGHTS

- Sausage King
- Carousel Bakery
- Mano's Deli
- Future Bakery
- Scheffler's Deli
- Alex Farm
- Caviar Direct

INFORMATION

- K8–K9; Locator map F3
- 92 Front Street East
- 416/392-7219; www.st.lawrence.to
- Tue–Thu 8–6, Fri 8–7, Sat 5–5
- King or Union
- King Street and Front Street streetcars
- Good
- Free
- St. James' Cathedral (➤ 56)

Distillery Historic District

HIGHLIGHTS

- Largest collection of Victorian industrial architecture in North America
- Heritage and architectural tour
- Microbrewery tour
- Film Buff tour (over 900 films shot here)

INFORMATION

- L9; Locator map off F3
- 55 Mill Street
- 416/364-1177; tours 416/597-0965; www. thedistillerydistrict.com
- Site opens 10am; stores, galleries and museums close 7pm Sun–Wed, 9pm Fri–Sat
- Many outlets
- Union Street, then 65 or 65A Parliament bus
- King 504 streetcar
- Good
- Free; tours moderate
- St. Lawrence Market (➤ 48)
- Various tours

Architecture buffs, art afficionados and gallery-hoppers head for a previously unloved part of town to an assemblage of Dickensian distillery buildings that has opened as Toronto's first planned artist district.

Where it began The seeds of William Gooderham's and James Worts' waterfront distillery were sown in 1837, and in just ten years became the world's largest distillery. In 1987, this outstanding example of Victorian industrial design was acquired by Allied Lyons who spent around $25 million on its preservation.

Everything old is new In December 2001, local visionary developers purchased the 13-acre (5ha) site and set about installing new life. Original concrete floors, brick walls and beamed ceilings remain unchanged. Over 340,000 old bricks from Cleveland have been laid in the lanes and alleyways, and a contemporary, creative group of tenants now inhabit the atmospheric buildings.

Arts and culture A jazz festival marked the opening in May 2003. Original distillery buildings now house a microbrewery making Ontario's first organic beer, museums like the Museum of Contemporary Canadian Art and over 30 art galleries, including two showing major international work—the Jane Corkin photography gallery and the Sandra Ainsley Glass Gallery, where there is a breathtaking collection of Dale Chihuly pieces. The Case Goods and Cannery Building holds about 50 studios and theater workshops and the Tank House has been transformed into a theater complex with indoor and outdoor stages. Ensconced in the Pump House is Balzac's Coffeehouse, where they roast and grind their own beans.

Ontario Science Centre

One of the first, and still one of the best of its kind, the Ontario Science Centre is a technological extravaganza. Make your way through the museum's different areas, learning as you tune in to more than 800 interactive exhibits.

High-tech halls Lively and challenging, the Science Centre is divided into 12 halls. Listen to a heart murmur in the Human Body Hall or send a probe into space in the Space Hall. The Sport Hall examines the games people play and the scientific principles involved, and in the Information Highway area, anyone can surf the Net. The Communication Hall deals with the science of human nature and offers games and tests that measure memory, intelligence and willingness to cooperate. The adage "You are what you eat" is explored in the Food Hall. A working weather station and a seismograph that lets you create a mini-earthquake are among the big draws in the Earth Hall. There's a working model of the world's first steam engine and a "bionic woman" with moveable parts in the Technology Hall, and in the Matter, Energy and Change area you can see yourself in infrared. The Science Arcade is filled with whirling, flashing exhibits exploring natural phenomena, while the Question of Truth Hall examines the impact bias, racism and sexism have had on scientific practice, and the Living Earth Hall focuses on ecology.

Omnimax The other great attraction is the Omnimax Theatre, a 79-ft (24m) dome screen with digital wraparound sound that creates the illusion of being in the thick of the movie action. You sit in a tilted-back position and watch a screen 10 times larger than the usual IMAX format.

HIGHLIGHTS

● Human Body Hall
● Space Hall
● Earth Hall
● Omnimax
● Rainforest

INFORMATION

✚ Off map to northeast; Locator map B1

✉ 770 Don Mills Road, North York at Eglinton

☎ 416/696-3127; www.ontarioscience centre.ca

🕐 Daily 10–5 (also until 8, Aug)

🍴 Restaurant, cafeteria

🚍 Pape then bus 25 north; Eglinton then bus 34 east; Kennedy then bus 34 west

♿ Very good

💲 Expensive

Toronto Zoo

HIGHLIGHTS

- The pavilions, especially *Edge of Night* in Australasia Pavilion
- Eurasia Outdoor Exhibits
- Americas Pavilion
- Re-created Maya temple
- Africa Pavilion

INFORMATION

- ✚ Off map to northeast; Locator map C1
- ✉ 361A Old Finch Avenue, Meadowvale Road, Scarborough
- ☎ 416/392-5900; www.torontozoo.com
- 🕐 Daily 9–7.30, May–Aug; 9–6, Mar–Apr, Sep–Oct; 9.30–4.30, Oct–Dec, rest of year
- 🍴 Two restaurants and four snackbars operated by McDonald's, plus picnic tables
- 🚇 Kennedy and then Scarborough bus 86A going east
- ♿ Very good
- 💲 Expensive
- ❓ "Meet the Keeper" program at various times and venues throughout the day

The 5,000 or so animals, representing 459 species, have much more freedom than many in similar institutions. Even their pavilions re-create their natural environment as closely as possible.

Australasia, Eurasia and the Americas Inspired by the San Diego Zoo, the 710 acres (287ha) are organized around eight pavilions and nearby outdoor paddocks. Inside each pavilion, a particular habitat and climate is replicated using flora, fauna and free-flying birds and butterflies. In the Australasia Pavilion you'll see bearded dragons, hairy-nosed wombats, kookaburras and Tasmanian devils, with kangaroos, wallabies and emus both inside and outside. The nearby Eurasia Outdoor Exhibits include the Siberian tiger, snow leopard and yak (plus camel rides). Frighteners in the Americas Pavilion include alligators, black widow spiders, boa constrictors, Mojave desert sidewinders and pink-toed tarantulas. Polar bears are outdoors, and nearby, at the re-created Maya temple, can be found the jaguar and a flock of flamingos.

Africa and the Indo-Malayan Pavilion Debrazza's and Patas monkeys chatter in the Africa Pavilion, which also houses the Gorilla Rainforest exhibit, home to silverback Charles and his family of seven. Outdoors, you can go on safari observing zebra, lion, giraffe, ostrich, cheetah, hyena, elephants, white rhinos and antelope. The orangutan and white-handed gibbon entertain in the Indo-Malaya Pavilion, along with hornbill and reticulated python. Near the pavilion are the Sumatran tigers, Indian rhinoceros, lion-tailed macaque and, in the Malayan Woods Pavilion, clouded leopard. In the Canadian Domain are a large herd of wood bison plus grizzly bear, wolf and cougar.

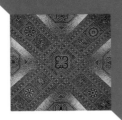

TORONTO's
best

Neighborhoods

THE ANNEX

In this residential neighborhood bordering the university, the homes (most built between 1880 and 1920) are populated by professionals, professors and journalists. Residents helped galvanize the opposition to the Spadina Expressway that would have blighted downtown. The strip of Bloor Street on its southern border is lined with coffee houses.
✚ H5–H6, J5–J6 ✉ Avenue Road to Bathurst and Bloor to Dupont
🚇 St. George or Spadina

THE BEACHES

At the eastern end of Queen Street, this is the district favored by baby boomers, attracted to the small-town atmosphere, the boardwalk along the lake and attractive Victorian homes along tree-shaded streets. Quirky stores, restaurants, cafés and antiques stores add interest to the attractive main street, Queen Street East.
✚ Off map to east 🚋 Queen Street East streetcar

Shop front at The Beaches

Vibrant Chinatown

CABBAGETOWN

Once described by Canadian author Hugh Garner as "the largest Anglo-Saxon slum in North America," this neighborhood of Victorian homes (between Wellesley and Dundas east of Sherbourne) has been thoroughly gentrified. The legend goes that it is so named because the front lawns were planted solid with cabbages by the early Irish immigrant residents in the 19th century.
✚ L7 🚋 Dundas, Wellesley or Carlton streetcar

CHINATOWN

Sprawling along Dundas and Spadina, the original Chinatown bustles day and night as people shop at stalls displaying brilliant green mustard and bok choy, fresh crabs and live fish, and herbal stores that sell "relaxing tea" and ginseng that costs hundreds of dollars for just one ounce. Today many of the businesses are operated by Thais and Vietnamese.
✚ H7 🚇 St. Patrick 🚋 Dundas streetcar

THE DANFORTH

Across the Don River Ravine east of Bloor, this Greek strip has become the city's late-night hot spot, where crowds jam the patios of the many bars and restaurants that line the sidewalk. If you come during the day you will find stores specializing in Greek goods, from foodstuffs to figurines.

N6 🚇 Chester or Pape

LITTLE ITALY

A vibrant Italian community thrives along College Street between Euclid and Shaw, where the street lamps bear neon maps of Italy. Old-fashioned cafés with hissing espresso and cappuccino machines operate alongside more modern, fashionable establishments. At night, in particular, the area buzzes with energy.

G7 🚋 College Street streetcar

QUEEN STREET WEST

This is where the hip hang out. It's where cabaret artist Holly Cole began her career and the Bamboo club introduced reggae and salsa to the city. Along this street between Simcoe and Bathurst are the outlets of young Canadian clothing designers, secondhand bookstores, fabric outlets and junk shops, all mixed up, in a neighborhood that has a very funky edge.

H8–J8 🚇 Osgoode 🚋 Queen Street West streetcar

ROSEDALE

Rosedale is Toronto's most affluent neighborhood, with large and beautiful homes owned by the city's movers and shakers.

K5 🚇 Rosedale

YORKVILLE

Once a village outside the city boundaries, in the 1960s this became Toronto's very own Haight-Ashbury before turning into the fashionable shopping scene that it is today. Designer names cluster in Hazelton Lanes and along Yorkville Avenue, and Bloor and Cumberland streets.

J6 🚇 Bloor-Yonge, Bay

SURBURBAN TORONTO

North York is an energetic area north of the city that features its own full complement of restaurants, shopping, theaters, galleries and other cultural institutions, plus a fun winter carnival. Etobicoke, pronounced "eh-toe-bi-coh," between the airport and downtown is mostly residential, but there are several excellent shopping centers and specialty shops in the neighborhood.
Scarborough is located east of downtown and includes the Scarborough Bluffs dramatic cliffs rising from Lake Ontario. There are wonderful hiking opportunities through the Rouge River Valley, and the famous Toronto Zoo (► 50) is here.

Yorkville

Modern Buildings

RAYMOND MORIYAMA

Raymond Moriyama (b1929) has given the city several striking buildings, each of which creatively resolves the restrictions of the site, at the same time carefully considering the surrounding environment. At Ontario Science Centre he took into account the ravine and the trees, while the Bata Shoe Museum is a perfect repository for the collection and sympathetic to surrounding buildings.

BCE PLACE

The whalebone-shaped galleria designed by architects Skidmore, Owings and Merrill with Bregman and Hamann is superb.

✚ J9 ✉ 181 Bay Street and Front ☎ 416/364-4693 🕐 Daily 🍴 Several 🚇 Union ♿ Good 💷 Free

EATON CENTRE

Enter at the southern end to see the splendor of Ed Zeidler's 866-ft (264m) long galleria and the sculptured flock of 60 Canada geese in flight by Michael Snow.

✚ J8–K8 ✉ Dundas and Yonge to Queen and Yonge ☎ 416/598-8700 🕐 Mon–Fri 10–9, Sat 9.30–7, Sun noon–6 🍴 Several restaurants plus food court 🚇 Dundas or Queen ♿ Very good 💷 Free

MASSEY COLLEGE

Built 1960–63, and designed by Ron Thom, the college features concertina-folded screen walls enclosing a quadrangle and fountain.

✚ J6 ✉ 4 Devonshire Place 🚇 Queen's Park 💷 Free

Roy Thomson Hall

METRO LIBRARY

Architect Raymond Moriyama flooded the library with natural light and gave it a pool and a waterfall.

✚ K6 ✉ 789 Yonge Street ☎ 416/393-7000 🕐 Mon–Thu 10–8, Fri–Sat 10–5, Sun 1.30–5 🚇 Bloor–Yonge ♿ Very good 💷 Free

ROYAL BANK PLAZA

The iridescent blaze on a summer day will dazzle your eyes; even when the weather is overcast, the distinctive shape of Webb Zerafa Menkes Housden's building will attract your attention.

✚ J9 ✉ Front and Bay streets 🍴 Several in concourse 🚇 Union ♿ Very good 💷 Free

ROY THOMSON HALL

This remarkable, flying-saucer-like creation is by Arthur Erickson; the concert hall has had a $2.4 million acoustics enhancement.

✚ J8–J9 ✉ 60 Simcoe Street ☎ 416/593-4828 🚇 St. Andrew ♿ Very good 💷 Free

Historic Buildings

Below: Campbell House

CAMPBELL HOUSE

The 1822 mansion of loyalist and sixth Chief Justice of Upper Canada, Sir William Campbell.
➕ J8 ✉ 160 Queen Street West ☎ 416/597-0227
🕐 Mon–Fri 9.30–4.30 (also Sat–Sun noon–4.30 in summer)
🚇 Osgoode 🚻 Few 💲 Moderate

COLBORNE LODGE

This 1836–37 Regency cottage and the surrounding acreage were donated to the city in 1873. Thus High Park was born (➤ 58).
➕ C 7 ✉ High Park ☎ 416/392-6916 🕐 Tue–Sun noon–5, mid-Apr to early Oct; noon–4, early Oct–Dec; Sat–Sun noon–4, rest of year
🚇 High Park 🚌 No. 501 streetcar 🚻 None 💲 Inexpensive

MACKENZIE HOUSE

This humble brick house was bought by friends for William Mackenzie, first mayor of Toronto and leader of the 1837 rebellion. He lived here 1859–61.
➕ K8 ✉ 82 Bond Street ☎ 416/392-6915 🕐 Tue–Sun noon–5 (Sat–Sun only in winter) 🚇 Dundas 🚻 Few 💲 Inexpensive

OLD CITY HALL

Today, Edward James Lennox's massive, Romanesque building houses the provincial courts.
➕ J8 ✉ 60 Queen Street West 🕐 Mon–Fri 9–5 🚇 Queen
🚻 Few 💲 Free

OSGOODE HALL

This building (1829) houses the headquarters of Ontario's legal profession, with an elegant interior and an impressive portrait and sculpture collection.
➕ J8 ✉ 130 Queen Street West ☎ 416/947-3300
🕐 Tours Mon–Fri at 1.15, Jul–Aug 🚇 Osgoode 🚻 Few
💲 Free

SPADINA HOUSE

The 1866 house retains its original furnishings and gas lights, plus many decorative objects.
➕ H5 ✉ 285 Spadina Road ☎ 416/392-6910 🕐 Daily noon–5, Jun–Aug; Tue–Fri noon–4, Sat–Sun noon–5, Apr–May, Sep; Sat–Sun noon–5, Jan–Mar 🚇 Dupont
🚻 Good 💲 Moderate

E. J. LENNOX (1855–1933)

Toronto born and educated, Edward James Lennox was one of the city's most influential architects, designing Old City Hall (1889), the west wing of the Provincial Parliament Buildings (1910) and Casa Loma (1914).

Above: Spadina House   55

Museums & Quiet Corners

Ned Hanlan *tugboat at The Pier*

MOUNT PLEASANT CEMETERY

Visit the graves of pianist Glenn Gould, the discoverers of insulin, Banting and Best, and Prime Minister Mackenzie King. Don't miss the extravagant mausoleums of the Massey and Eaton families.

✚ K3–L3 ✉ 1643 Yonge Street or 375 Mount Pleasant Road ☎ 416/485-9129 🕐 Daily 8–dusk 🚇 St. Clair ♿ Good 💲 Free

MUSEUM FOR TEXTILES

This gem of a museum has changing exhibitions. Each offers collections that are guaranteed to be esthetically engaging as well as of anthropological interest.

✚ J8 ✉ 55 Centre Avenue ☎ 416/599-5321 🕐 Tue–Fri 11–5 (Wed to 8); Sat–Sun noon–5 🚇 St. Patrick ♿ Good 💲 Moderate

THE NECROPOLIS

Beyond the charming porte-cochere and Gothic Revival chapel lie 15 acres (6ha) of hallowed ground containing many historical figures, including William Lyon Mackenzie and famous oarsman Ned Hanlan.

✚ L7–M7 ✉ 200 Winchester Street at Sumach Street ☎ 416/923-7911 🕐 Daily 8–dusk 🚇 Castle Frank ♿ Good 💲 Free

THE PIER

This museum tells the story of the lake and the men and ships that plied it. In summer, you can go aboard the *Ned Hanlan* tugboat (1932).

✚ J9 ✉ 245 Queens Quay ☎ 416/338-7437 🕐 Daily 10–6, Jul–Aug; 10–4, rest of year 🚇 LRT or 510 ♿ Few 💲 Moderate

TWO UNIVERSITY ART GALLERIES

The University of Toronto Art Centre (✚ J6–J7 ✉ 15 King's College Circle ☎ 416/978-1838) displays the Lillian Malcove Medieval Collection, which includes the 1538 *Adam and Eve* by Lucas Cranach. It also includes some drawings by Pablo Picasso, Paul Klee and Henri Matisse. Hart House has a fine collection of contemporary Canadian art throughout the building and in the Justina M. Barnicke Art Gallery (✚ J6–J7 ✉ 7 Hart House Circle ☎ 416/978-8398).

ST. JAMES' CATHEDRAL

The present building was finished in 1874, but there was an earlier frame building that served as York's first church. In the beautiful interior, note the Tiffany window at the northern end of the east aisle in memory of William Jarvis.

✚ K8 ✉ 65 Church Street at King ☎ 416/364-7865 🚇 King ♿ Good 💲 Free

Spectator Sports & Activities

--- In the Top 25 ---

12 SKYDOME (▶ 36)

BASEBALL—THE BLUE JAYS

World Series champions in 1992 and 1993, the team attracts 4 million fans each season.

➕ H9–J9 ✉ 1 Blue Jays Way, Suite 3200 ☎ Administration 416/341-1000; tickets 416/341-1234 🚇 Union 💵 Expensive

BASKETBALL—THE RAPTORS

The purple dinosaur that you see everywhere in the city is the mascot of Toronto's basketball team, the Raptors, who appear at the Air Canada Centre.

➕ H9 ✉ 20 Bay Street, Suite 1702 ☎ Administration 416/815-5600 🚇 Union 💵 Expensive

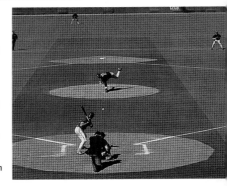

BIKING

Toronto has 50 miles (80km) of bike routes. The Martin Goodman Trail runs along the waterfront. Bicycles can be rented at various venues.

CANOEING/KAYAKING/SAILING

Queen's Quay Yachting ✉ 283 Queen's Quay West ☎ 416/203-3000 rents out sail and powerboats, and organizes sailing courses. The Harbourfront Canoe and Kayak School ✉ 283A Queen's Quay West ☎ 416/203-2277 rents out kayaks and canoes. Boats can be rented on the Toronto Islands.

GOLF

The Bell Canadian Open has been held on Canada's Labour Day (first Mon Sep) at Glen Abbey Golf Club in Oakville. Two worthy Metro courses are Humber Valley ✉ Rexdale ☎ 416/392-2488 and Tam O'Shanter ✉ Birchmount Avenue, Scarborough ☎ 416/392-2547

HOCKEY—THE MAPLE LEAFS

The Leafs played their last game at Maple Leaf Gardens in February 1999. Now you can witness Canadians succumbing to hockey fever at Air Canada Centre. Alas, tickets are almost impossible to obtain.

➕ K7 ✉ 60 Carlton Street ☎ 416/977-1641 🚇 College 💵 Expensive

ICE SKATING

In winter, Torontonians head for the rink in front of City Hall, to Harbourfront or to Grenadier Pond in High Park, where a bonfire glows and chestnuts roast.

Blue Jays playing at the SkyDome

A TRIO OF SPORTS TRIVIA

1. No matter what others may tell you, basketball was invented by a Canadian, James A. Naismith from Almonte, Ontario, in 1891.

2. Before breaking into the major baseball leagues, Babe Ruth hit his first home run as a professional player at a game played on 15 September, 1914, at Hanlan's Point Stadium on the Toronto Islands.

3. Lacrosse, not hockey, is Canada's national game.

Green Spaces

ALLAN GARDENS

The glass-domed Palm House, modeled on the one at Kew Gardens in London, still stands here in radiant Victorian glory.

➕ K7 ✉ Between Jarvis, Sherbourne, Carlton and Gerrard streets ☎ 416/392-7288 🕐 Mon–Fri 9–4, Sat–Sun 10–5 🚇 College ♿ Good 🎫 Free

Spring flowers at Edwards Gardens

EDWARDS GARDENS

This formal garden is popular in spring and summer, especially at rhododendron time. Tours leave from the Civic Garden Centre.

➕ Off map to northwest ✉ Lawrence Avenue and Leslie Street ☎ 416/397-1340 🕐 Daily dawn to dusk 🚇 Eglinton and then Leslie or Lawrence bus ♿ Good 🎫 Free

HIGH PARK

This 395-acre (160ha) park is the city playground. People bike, jog, stroll, picnic, swim in the pool and play games on the sports fields. Grenadier Pond becomes a skating rink in winter.

➕ C6–C7 ✉ Bloor Street West and Parkside Drive ☎ 416/392-1111 🕐 Daily dawn to dusk 🍴 Snack bars 🚇 High Park ♿ Good 🎫 Free

THE RAVINES

There are 21 of these parks in Toronto. Wooded and cut with streams, they shelter abundant natural life and offer great opportunities for birdwatching. At the Glen Stewart Ravine, which runs from Kingston Road and Glen Manor Road south toward Queen Street East, you can stroll the nature trail and see cardinals, chickadees, indigo buntings and many other species.

KORTWRIGHT CENTRE FOR CONSERVATION

In 400 acres (160ha) of the Humber River Valley: 11 miles (18km) of trails, with guided walks, exhibits and videos.

➕ Off map to northwest ✉ In Vaughan ☎ 416/661-6600 🕐 Daily 10–4 🍴 Café ♿ Good 🎫 Free

QUEEN'S PARK

Extending in front and behind the provincial buildings; studded with statues of local heroes.

➕ J6 ✉ College and Avenue Road 🕐 Daily 🚇 Queen's Park ♿ Good 🎫 Free

TOMMY THOMPSON PARK

On an artificial peninsula extending into Lake Ontario, this park provides a nesting habitat for 29 bird species. Interpretive programs are offered on weekends and holidays in summer.

➕ Off map to southeast ✉ At end of Leslie Street on waterfront ☎ 416/661-6600 🕐 Sat, Sun, holidays 9–6 🚇 Leslie and Commissioners streets, then free shuttle ♿ Few 🎫 Free

For Kids

In the Top 25

13 ART GALLERY OF ONTARIO (► 38)
4 BLACK CREEK PIONEER VILLAGE (► 29)
3 PARAMOUNT CANADA'S WONDERLAND (► 28)
12 CN TOWER (► 37)
6 FORT YORK (► 31)
16 HARBOURFRONT (► 43)
20 THE HOCKEY HALL OF FAME (► 45)
25 TORONTO ZOO (► 50)
5 ONTARIO PLACE (► 30)
24 ONTARIO SCIENCE CENTRE (► 49)
15 ROYAL ONTARIO MUSEUM (► 40)
21 THE TORONTO ISLANDS (► 46)

THAT'S ENTERTAINMENT

The city offers an astonishing array of children's entertainment. Many take place at Harbourfront, like the Saturday afternoon Cushion Concerts (for 5- to 12-year-olds), creative crafts on Sundays, daycamps during school breaks, plus the seven-day Milk International Festival of music, dance, theater and puppetry in May.

AFRICAN LION SAFARI

Look out for lions, tigers and other game in this 500-acre (200ha) wildlife park, ride the *African Queen* or the scenic railroad, and see animal performances. There are playgrounds too.
➕ Off map to southwest ✉ R R No. 1, Cambridge. Take Hwy 401 to Hwy 6 south ☎ 519/623-2620 🕐 Daily 9–7.30, May–Aug; 9–6, Mar–Apr, Sep–Oct; 9.30–4.30, rest of year 🍴 Cafeteria/snack bar 💷 Expensive

PLAYDIUM

A good selection of interactive games and simulators, rock-climbing walls, karting track, batting cages, IMAX theater.
➕ Off map to west ✉ 99 Rathburn Road West, Mississauga ☎ 905/273-9000 🕐 Mon–Thu noon–midnight, Fri noon–2am, Sat 10am–2am, Sat 10am–midnight 🍴 Restaurant, café 🚇 Islington then bus No. 20 ♿ Good 💷 Prices vary

RIVERDALE FARM

Early 20th-century farm by the Don Valley Ravine.
➕ L7–M7 ✉ 201 Winchester Street ☎ 416/392-6794 🕐 Daily 9–5 🚇 Carlton streetcar 💷 Free

WILDWATER KINGDOM

A huge water theme park with a wave pool, slides, giant hot tubs—and the Cyclone water ride.
➕ Off map to northwest ✉ Finch Avenue, 1 mile (0.6km) west of Hwy 427, Brampton ☎ 416/369-0123 or 905/794-0565 🕐 Daily 10am–11pm, mid-Jun to Labour Day (water rides until 8); Sat–Sun 10–6, May to mid-Jun 🍴 Three restaurants ♿ Few 💷 Expensive

YOUNG PEOPLE'S THEATRE

Presents adaptations of Charles Dickens, Clive Staples Lewis and other authors' stories from October to May.
➕ K8–K9 ✉ 165 Front Street East, at Sherbourne Street ☎ Box office 416/862-2222; administration 416/363-5131 🚇 Union, King ♿ Good 💷 Prices vary

Taking the weight of the world on his shoulders

59

Galleries

BAU-XI

Paintings, sculpture, drawings and prints by such contemporary Canadian artists as Jack Shadbolt and Hugh Mackenzie.

🚩 H8 ✉ 80 Spadina Avenue at King Street ☎ 416/977-0600 🕔 Tue–Sat 10–5.30 🚃 King streetcar to Spadina 🎟 Free

Mask, Bay of Spirits Gallery

INUIT ART SPECIALISTS

Eskimo Art Gallery (🚩 J9 ✉ 12 Queen's Quay West ☎ 416/366-3000) has high-quality Inuit sculptures with prices starting as low as Can$40. Isaacs/Inuit Gallery (🚩 H6–J6 ✉ 9 Prince Arthur Avenue ☎ 416/921-9985) is a leading specialist in Arctic art and early Native Canadian art and artifacts. Feheley Fine Arts (🚩 J5 ✉ 14 Hazelton Avenue ☎ 416/323-1373) has exhibited and sold Inuit art for more than 30 years.

BAY OF SPIRITS GALLERY

Totem poles, masks, prints and jewelry by the Native Indians of the Pacific Coast.
🚩 J9 ✉ 156 Front Street West ☎ 416/971-5190 🕔 Mon–Fri 10–6, Sat 11–5 🚃 Front streetcar 🎟 Free

GALLERY ONE

After more than 20 years on the city art scene, the gallery represents a raft of Canadian artists such as Jack Bush, Kenneth Lockhead and Americans such as Helen Frankenthaler and Stanley Boxer.
🚩 J6 ✉ 121 Scollard Street ☎ 416/929-3103 🕔 Tue–Sat 10.30–5 🚃 Bay 🎟 Free

JANE CORKIN

A major photographic gallery that deals in both historical and contemporary photographs.
🚩 J8 ✉ 179 John Street ☎ 416/979-1980 🕔 Mon–Fri 9.30–5.30, Sat 10–5 🚃 Osgoode 🎟 Free

MIRA GODARD

A major gallery representing such names as Fernando Botero, Robert Motherwell, Frank Stella, David Hockney, Jasper Johns and Lawren Harris.
🚩 J6 ✉ 22 Hazelton Avenue ☎ 416/964-8197 🕔 Tue–Sat 10–5.30 🚃 Bay 🎟 Free

MOOSE FACTORY GALLERY

Charles Pachter is one of Canada's leading contemporary artists. His portrait of Queen Elizabeth II on a moose is an icon of Canadian pop art. This exhibit has new paintings, sculpture, books and cards.
🚩 H8 ✉ 22 Grange Avenue ☎ 416/596-8452 for appointment 🚃 Osgoode 🎟 Free

NANCY POOLE'S STUDIO

Another veteran on the art scene representing a roster of 25 or so contemporary artists. Mounts fine single artist shows. Group shows often in summer.
🚩 J6 ✉ 16 Hazelton Avenue ☎ 416/964-9050 🕔 Tue–Sat 10–5 🚃 Bay 🎟 Free

Public & Outdoor Art

In the Top 25

🔟 **CITY HALL (➤ 44)**

CITY HALL

Many of the works that once graced Metro Hall have been moved into City Hall and can be seen scattered throughout the building.

➕ J8 ✉ Queen Street West ☎ 416/338-0338 🚇 Queen or Osgoode ✋ Free

GUILD INN

Historic architectural fragments dot the grounds of the Guild Inn, including a white marble façade from the Imperial Bank of Canada building. Enjoy brunch or cocktails on the veranda and stroll through the grounds to the Scarborough Bluffs.

➕ Off map to northeast ✉ 201 Guildwood Parkway, Scarborough ☎ 416/261-3331 🚇 Kennedy ✋ Free

MURAL ON THE "FLAT IRON" BUILDING

Approach the Gooderham or "flat iron" building (1892) from the west and you are faced with a strange mural by Derek Besant, installed in 1980. You can make of it what you will.

➕ K9 ✉ 49 Wellington Street East at Church 🚇 Union ✋ Free

PASTURE

Tucked away in a courtyard by the Aetna Centre, several stolid cows by Joe Fafard sit in a pasture, a reminder that Toronto's wealth was originally derived from farming.

➕ J9 ✉ Aetna Centre/TDC 🚇 King ✋ Free

PRINCESS OF WALES THEATRE

The interior murals and other elements designed by Frank Stella are stunning for those who pay money to attend a performance at this state-of-the-art theater. But the exterior back wall's explosion of color and abstraction is free to all.

➕ J8 ✉ 300 King Street West 🚇 St. Andrew ✋ Free

THREE WAY PIECE NUMBER TWO

In front of City Hall stands an abstract form by Henry Moore. Known more commonly as *The Archer*, it suggests both solidity and flexibility.

➕ J8 ✉ Nathan Phillips Square 🚇 Osgoode ✋ Free

SKYDOME'S GARGOYLES

The figures leaning out from the SkyDome (➤ 36) like modern gargoyles were fashioned by Michael Snow, who also created the flock of geese in the Eaton Centre (➤ 54, 72). The 15 figures, all in different postures of elation or despair, make up *The Audience*. They have been coated with weather-resistant fiberglass and covered with a bronze-like metallic paint.

Henry Moore sculpture at City Hall

61

What's Free

ALL FREE

Gardens, parks, markets, churches, political debates, industrial tours and cemeteries are free. So are some walking tours, like those at the university or those led by the Toronto Historical Board. Also free in summer, swimming at a municipal pool, and the theater in High Park. Visit the Royal Ontario Museum (▶ 40) free of charge on Friday evenings between 4.30 and 9.30.

CBC BUILDING

In the grand atrium you can see radio hosts speaking into microphones and technicians keeping everyone on track. The little museum is fun and free. Enjoy a variety of clips from radio and TV, and take the free tour to see studios and sets, maybe cruising the racks of the awesome costume department, where everything is organized by period or decade.
➕ J9 ✉ 250 Front Street West ☎ 416/205-8605 ⏰ Tour times vary 🍴 Cafeteria 🚇 Union ♿ Good

CHUM/CITYTV

This is as far from CBC as you can possibly get. Toronto's radical media company doesn't have fixed studios: cameras roll wherever they are needed—on the roof, in the hallways, even outside. Extreme haircuts or pierced body parts are far from shocking; knowing what's hip is what matters. This is the station where you can air your gripes and have them put out on prime time if they're colorful enough. Despite the "anything goes" attitude, reservations are necessary for the very popular free tours, which are often filled six months in advance.
➕ J8 ✉ 299 Queen Street West ☎ 416/591-5757 ⏰ Tour times vary 🚇 Osgoode

TORONTO STOCK EXCHANGE

All trading is now electronic. The building houses a museum with interactive displays about stocks and finances, and the Design Exchange, promoting the newest and best Canadian design.
➕ J8 ✉ Exchange Tower, 2 First Canadian Place at King and York Streets ☎ 416/947-4670 ⏰ Call for tour times 🚇 King

WALKING THE NEIGHBORHOODS

Some of the best free entertainment is out on the streets. Chinatown (▶ 52) is colorful and there is plenty to look at in Queen Street West (▶ 53). For natural beauty, stroll around the Harbourfront (▶ 43) or visit The Beaches (▶ 52). A trip to the Toronto Islands (▶ 46), though not free, costs very little and takes you to another world—water, peace and quiet.

STREETCAR RIDING

Maybe not free, but it's very inexpensive to ride a streetcar, and you are assured of great visual entertainment. Among the best lines are Queen Street, College and Dundas.

Mural at the Toronto Stock Exchange

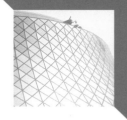

TORONTO
where to...

Neighborhood Favorites

PRICES

Expect to pay per person for a meal, excluding drink

$	up to Can$30
$$	up to Can$50
$$$	over Can$50

MORE LOCAL FAVORITES

Taro Grill (🕂 H8 ✉ 492 Queen Street West ☎ 416/504-1320) is hip. **Grappa** (🕂 H7 ✉ 797 College ☎ 416/535-3337) is rustic Italian. **Messis** (🕂 H6 ✉ 97 Harbord ☎ 416/920-2186) offers contemporary Northern Italian cuisine. **Herbs** (✉ 3187 Yonge ☎ 416/322-0487) is bistro at its best. All are small and serve good, reasonably priced food.

A FEW TIPS

Restaurant checks (bills) include a 7 percent goods and service tax (GST), and 8 percent provincial sales tax (PST), which together equal 15 percent tax. Always tip on the pre-tax total of the check. Most restaurants are smoke free. Call first if this is important to you. Well-dressed casual is acceptable in most restaurants. Men might feel more comfortable wearing a jacket in the more upscale dining spots.

THE ANNEX

BISTRO TOURNESOL ($)

Classic fixed-price French bistro serving mouth-watering pâtés, steamed salmon, steak frites and crème brûlée.
🕂 H5 ✉ 406 Dupont Street ☎ 416/921-7766 ⊕ Dinner only; closed Mon 🚇 Dupont

DOWNTOWN

KITKAT ($$)

A theater district clientele of journalists and TV and movie people eat honey-garlic backribs, pasta dishes and lemon chicken amid cat memorabilia and old movie posters.
🕂 H8 ✉ 297 King Street West ☎ 416/977-4461 ⊕ Lunch Mon–Fri; dinner Mon–Sat 🚇 St. Andrew

TORCH BISTRO ($$)

Draw the velvet curtains for privacy in a booth, or choose comfy leather banquettes in early 20th century bistro style. The steak frites, roast duck and rich oceanic bouillabaisse are particularly special.
🕂 K8 ✉ 253 Victoria Street ☎ 416/364-7517 ⊕ Dinner Tue–Sun 🚇 Dundas or Queen

LITTLE ITALY

TRATTORIA GIANCARLO ($$)

Small and intimate in Little Italy. People come for the perfectly grilled dishes and the superlative pastas and risottos.
🕂 G7 ✉ 41–43 Clinton Street at College ☎ 416/533-9619 ⊕ Dinner Mon–Sat 6–11 🚇 College Street streetcar

QUEEN STREET WEST

CITIES BISTRO ($)

Home to a hip and savvy crowd who know great value when they taste it—Asian-accented dishes such as black tiger shrimp and pineapple salsa.
🕂 G8 ✉ 859 Queen Street West ☎ 416/504-3762 ⊕ Lunch Tue–Fri; dinner daily 🚇 Queen Street West streetcar

LE SELECT ($$)

Bistro fare at moderate prices. Typical dishes are *bavette aux échalotes* and duck confit. Patio with jazz playing in the background.
🕂 H8 ✉ 328 Queen Street West ☎ 416/596-6405 ⊕ Mon–Thu 11.30am–11.30pm, Fri–Sat 11.30am–midnight, Sun noon–10.30 🚇 Queen Street West streetcar

ROSEDALE

BROWNE'S BISTRO ($$)

The well-heeled Rosedale crowd enjoy fine cooking in the modern Italian vein. Lamb dishes are special here.
🕂 K4 ✉ 4 Woodlawn Avenue East ☎ 416/924-8132 ⊕ Lunch Mon–Fri; dinner daily 🚇 Summerhill

YORKVILLE

LE PARADIS ($)

French bistro on a budget. Good, well priced wines. Herb-roasted chicken, steak frites and a superb fixed-price menu.
🕂 J6 ✉ 166 Bedford Road ☎ 416/921-0995 ⊕ Lunch Tue–Fri; dinner daily 🚇 St. George

Noted for Cuisine

AVALON ($$$)
Inspired cuisine by top young chef Christopher McDonald. Small, elegant and comfortable. Simple, full-flavored food with favorites like herb-roasted chicken and rib steak with horseradish sauce.
✚ J8 ✉ 270 Adelaide Street West at John ☎ 416/979-9918 🕘 Lunch Wed–Fri; dinner Mon–Sat 🚇 Osgoode or St. Andrew

BOBA ($$$)
Innovative cuisine mixing different ethnic flavors (rice paper wrapped chicken breast with rice wine vinegar sauce).
✚ J5 ✉ 90 Avenue Road ☎ 416/961-2622 🕘 Dinner Mon–Sat 🚇 Bay or St. George

CENTRO ($$$)
Contemporary French-Italian cuisine superbly prepared and presented.
✚ K1 ✉ 2472 Yonge Street ☎ 416/483-2211 🕘 Dinner Mon–Sat 🚇 Eglinton

HEMISPHERES ($$$)
At this hotel dining room, watch the chefs through the window wall of the vast kitchen as they put an exciting East-West spin on fine ingredients. Flawless grilled fish, veal tenderloin dressed to the nines and a sumptuous fresh menu.
✚ J8 ✉ Metropolitan Hotel, 110 Chestnut Street ☎ 416/599-8000 🕘 Lunch Mon–Sat; dinner Tue–Sat 🚇 Dundas

NORTH 44 ($$$)
Excels in melding a variety of international flavors—try the rack of lamb with pecan mustard crust and Zinfandel sauce. Dramatic art deco-style room. Upstairs wine bar.
✚ K1 ✉ 2537 Yonge Street ☎ 416/487-4897 🕘 Dinner Mon–Sat 🚇 Eglinton 🚌 97X

SCARAMOUCHE ($$$)
Imaginative use of ingredients and flavors especially in the accompaniments (such as caramelized onions with sautéed artichoke hearts, eggplant, leek and roasted peppers). Pasta Bar has a bistro menu.
✚ J4 ✉ 1 Benvenuto Place (off Edmond Avenue, south of St. Clair) ☎ 416/961-8011 🕘 Dinner Mon–Sat 🚇 St. Clair

SUSUR ($$$)
The darling of fusion cuisine, chef Susur Lee's dishes are complete gastronomic poetry. Look especially for the rack of baby lamb with green curry sauce. The Chinese Wuxi pork is lushly sauced and slow cooked. Desserts are also a delight.
✚ K1 ✉ 601 King Street West ☎ 416/603-2205 🕘 Dinner Mon–Sat 🚇 King Street streetcar Westbound

TRUFFLES ($$$)
Toronto's premier hotel dining room, and probably one of the best restaurants in North America. The cuisine is fresh, unusual and flavorful, the interior design is in simple but luxurious good taste.
✚ J6 ✉ Four Seasons Hotel, 21 Avenue Road ☎ 416/964-0411 🕘 Dinner Mon–Sat 🚇 Bay

MORE GOURMET SPOTS

The most legendary dining is found outside town at **Eigensinn Farm** (☎ 519/922-3128), where genius chef Michael Stadtländer presents four-hour-long dinners. Other food favorites include:
YYZ ✉ 345 Adelaide Street West ☎ 416/599-3399
Reds Bistro & Bar ✉ 77 Adelaide Street West ☎ 416/862-7337
Crush ✉ 455 King Street West ☎ 416/977-1234
Brasserie Aix ✉ 584 College Street ☎ 416/588-7377
Xacutti ✉ 503 College Street ☎ 416/323-3957

Outdoor Patios

LAKEFRONT DINING

For a lakefront seat, check out Harbourfront (➤ 44). In Queen's Quay, Spinnakers and the Boathouse Café both have outdoor terraces. At the eastern end of the harbor you can dine aboard a cruise ship at **Captain John's** (✚ K9 ☎ 416/363-6062), while farther west along the docks, **Pier 4** (✚ J9 ☎ 416/203-5865) and **Wallymagoo's Marine Bar** (✚ J9 ☎ 416/203-6248) both attract lovers of fish and shellfish. Best of all, though, for a real-down-on-the-lakefront dining experience, bring your own picnic.

ALICE FAZOOLI'S ($$)

The patio is warmed by a fire and beautified by a fountain and gardenias, and often features live bands. Inside, the main draws are crabs and raw bar specialties.

✚ H8 ✉ 294 Adelaide Street West ☎ 416/979-1910 🕐 Lunch and dinner daily 🚇 Osgoode or St. Andrew

BYMARK ($$$)

Dramatic decor of wood, glass and water with a delectable menu of classic favorites and service to match. A bar one floor up offers extreme comfort and a great view. Summer patio.

✚ J9 ✉ 66 Wellington Street West ☎ 416/777-1145 🕐 Mon–Fri 11.30am–midnight, Sat 5pm–midnight 🚇 Union

COURT HOUSE MARKET GRILLE AND CHAMBER LOUNGE ($$)

At this 1852 stone courthouse you'll find a plain-language menu of grills and rotisseries. After your meal take a tour of the hanging area and the old jail cells.

✚ K8 ✉ 57 Adelaide Street East ☎ 416/214-9379 🕐 Lunch Mon–Fri; dinner daily 🚇 King

FLOW BAR & GRILL ($)

A smart new restaurant in the heart of Yorkville. Comfort, affordability and dishes designed for today's lifestyle are the key.

✚ J6 ✉ 133 Yorkville ☎ No phone 🕐 Breakfast, lunch and dinner daily 🚇 Museum or Bay

JUMP CAFÉ/BAR ($$)

Eclectic cuisine ranges from pizzas to chicken breast flavored with honey rosemary, and balsamic vinegar. The patio looks out over Commerce Court.

✚ J8 ✉ 1 Wellington Street West ☎ 416/363-3400 🕐 Lunch Mon–Fri; dinner Mon–Sat 🚇 King

MESSIS ($$)

The lights on the romantic patio wink an invitation to dine on penne with smoked chicken and mushrooms, sage-marinated veal loin and oven-roasted Atlantic salmon.

✚ H6 ✉ 97 Harbord Street ☎ 416/920-2186 🕐 Dinner daily 🚇 Spadina

SOUTHERN ACCENT ($$)

In Markham Village, with a spacious canopy-covered brick patio. Gumbo, jambalaya, blackened fish and other spicy dishes from Louisiana. Finish with bread pudding and bourbon sauce.

✚ G6 ✉ 595 Markham Street ☎ 416/536-3211 🕐 Dinner daily; lunch summer only 🚇 Bathurst

STARFISH ($$)

The owner of this comfy, neat restaurant is a walking encyclopedia of oyster and seafood lore. An array of oysters, oven roasted black cod and east coast lobsers will make you fall for Starfish hook, line and sinker.

✚ K8 ✉ 200 Adelaide Street East ☎ 416/366-7827 🕐 Mon–Fri lunch and dinner, Sat dinner only 🚇 King

Traditional Canandian

BLOOR STREET DINER ($)

Serving shoppers and late-nighters, it combines an espresso bar, a rotisserie where meats, poultry and fish are prepared in Provençal style and a *café-terrasse* (a great place to relax in summer).

➕ J6 ✉ 55 Bloor Street West in the Manulife Centre ☎ 416/928-3105 🕐 Daily 7am–1am 🚇 Bay or Bloor-Yonge

CANOE ($$$)

On the 54th floor of the TDC building. Inventive cuisine making use of Canadian ingredients (Digby scallops, Alberta beef, Grandview venison).

➕ J8–9 ✉ 66 Wellington Street West ☎ 416/364-0054 🕐 Lunch and dinner Mon–Fri 🚇 Union

HARBOUR SIXTY STEAK HOUSE ($$$)

Up stone steps to a baroque-inspired foyer to enjoy the finest basic foodstuffs. Prime beef, tuna steaks, lobsters on ice, Atlantic salmon and the best slow-roasted prime rib beef in town.

➕ J9 ✉ 60 Harbour Street ☎ 416/777-2111 🕐 Lunch Mon–Fri; dinner daily. 🚇 Union

JOSO'S ($$)

The best place for fresh fish in Toronto. Select your own fish from the tray and it will be grilled, steamed, poached, or cooked in any way to please your palate. The calamari are legendary. Interior created by the owner, singer-entertainer Joseph Spralja.

➕ J5 ✉ 202 Davenport Road (just east of Avenue Road)

☎ 416/925-1903 🕐 Lunch Mon–Fri; dinner Mon–Sat 🚇 Bay 🚌 Bus 6

MONTREAL ($$)

Serves such Quebecois favorites as pea soup and *tourtière* (a meat pie), plus terrific jazz next door.

➕ K8 ✉ 65 Sherbourne Street (at Adelaide) ☎ 416/363-0179 🕐 Lunch Mon–Fri; dinner Mon–Sat 🚇 Queen or King 🚋 Queen Street East streetcar

PANGAEA ($$$)

Tranquility and huge floral arrangements create an air of luxury here. Sophisticated cooking, with velvety soups and a French/Italian menu. A favorite with the entertainment biz. A delicious afternoon tea also available.

➕ J6 ✉ 1221 Bay Street ☎ 416/920-2323 🕐 Lunch and dinner Mon–Sat 🚇 Bay

RODNEY'S OYSTER HOUSE ($$)

As close as you'll get, in Toronto, to a traditional Nova Scotia seafood shack, with steamed delicacies.

➕ K8 ✉ 209 Adelaide Street East ☎ 416/363-8105 🕐 Lunch and dinner Mon–Sat 🚇 King

SHOPSY'S ($)

One of the few delis left in Toronto, and the place to come for a thick pastrami or good corned beef sandwich.

➕ K9 ✉ 33 Yonge Street ☎ 416/365-3333 🕐 Mon–Wed 7am–11pm, Thu–Fri 7am–midnight, Sat 8am–midnight, Sun 8am–11pm 🚇 Union

LOCAL ONTARIO WINES

Ever since the VQA (Vintners' Quality Alliance) appellation was introduced in 1988, Ontario's wines have improved immensely, and now you will find them on the very best wine lists. Look for Cave Spring, Konzelmann, Stoney Ridge and the big names—Inniskillin, Château des Charmes and Hillebrand. Canada's ice wine is internationally known. Made from grapes that have frozen on the vine, it is thick, rich and sweet—delicious with *biscotti*.

Decked Out in Style

MOVENPICK: NO EXPENSE SPARED

It took $6.5 million to create Movenpick's Palavrion (✉ 270 Front Street West ☎ 416/979-0060), a two-story stage set featuring hand painted tiles on the floors and walls, extravagant lighting fixtures and *trompe l'oeil* art. Eye-catching displays of fruits, vegetables, pastries and other foodstuffs decorate Movenpick's Marché in the BCE Galleria (☎ 416/366-8986), where you can eat at tables set under artificial trees.

AUBERGE DU POMMIER ($$$)

A romantic French country-style *auberge* with the gardens, stone and architecture to match. The food tends to be a little fussy, though.
✚ Off map to north ✉ 4150 Yonge Street at York Mills ☎ 416/222-2220 ◉ Lunch Mon–Fri; dinner Mon–Sat ⦿ York Mills

BISTRO 990 ($$$)

Informality and a superior kitchen combine to make this one of the hottest tickets in town for locals and stars working in "Hollywood North." A friendly welcome, attentive service and a menu featuring Provençal cuisine favorites explains why.
✚ J6 ✉ 990 Bay Street ☎ 416/921-9990 ◉ Lunch and dinner daily ⦿ Bay

COURTYARD CAFÉ ($$$)

An impressive three-story dining room with dramatic columns, balconies and chandeliers, caught between the formality of Europe and the pizzazz of California. Foie gras done in two different ways, outstanding grills, roasts and divine desserts.
✚ J6 ✉ Windsor Arms Hotel, 18 St. Thomas Street ☎ 416/971-9666 ◉ Lunch daily; dinner Tue–Sat ⦿ Bay

THE MARCHÉ ($)

A vast indoor European market with the world's foods made to order before your very eyes at cooking stations. There's an in-house bakery. Fill up your tray and dine in any one of seven themed seating areas.
✚ J9 ✉ 42 Yonge Street (in BCE Place) ☎ 416/366-8986 ◉ Breakfast, lunch and dinner daily ⦿ Union

MORTON'S OF CHICAGO ($$$)

A steakhouse that is always a cut above the rest. The menu features United States Department of Agriculture (USDA) rated prime beef—the very best from south of the border.
✚ J6 ✉ 4 Avenue Road ☎ 416/925-0648 ◉ Dinner daily ⦿ Bay or Museum

SENSES ($$$)

Sophisticated, clean lines are the hallmark of this 40-seat restaurant in the city's newest luxury hotel. Signature dishes favor triple searing of meats. Pristine cooking gives us fish poached in seaweed broth. Desserts to die for.
✚ H9 ✉ Soho Metropolitan Hotel, 328 Wellington Street West ☎ 416/961-0119 ◉ Dinner only Tue–Sat ⦿ Union 🚋 King streetcar

SPLENDIDO ($$$)

Sophisticated Toronto style where burnished wood and mirrors set the mood. The chef creates vignettes of land and sea; wine braised ox tail, whole fish roasted in wood burning ovens and duet of duckling, plus dreamy desserts.
✚ H6 ✉ 88 Harbord Street ☎ 416/929-7788 ◉ Dinner Tue–Sun ⦿ Spadina

Coffee, Cakes & Light Bites

ALLEN'S ($)
A vintage, New York-style saloon complete with oak bar stocking over 45 imported or microbrewed beers. Burgers, grilled chicken, fish and chips and pasta served with panache. A backyard barbecue opens in summer.
➕ M6 ✉ 143 Danforth Avenue ☎ 416/463-3086 🕐 Mon–Fri 11.30am–1.30am, Sat, Sun 11am–2am
🚇 Broadview

BAR ITALIA ($)
Italian chic with an upstairs pool hall and a downstairs café jammed at night with a young crowd.
➕ G7 ✉ 582 College Street ☎ 416/535-3621 🕐 Mon–Thu 11.30am–11.30pm, Fri 11.30am–12.30am, Sat 9.30am–12.30am, Sun 9.30am–11.30pm
🚋 College Street streetcar

BREGMAN'S BAKERY RESTAURANT ($)
Irresistible bagels, cakes, cookies and muffins. Full deli dining room upstairs with salads, big sandwiches, pasta and stirfrys.
➕ K4 ✉ 1560 Yonge Street ☎ 416/967-2750 🕐 Breakfast, lunch and dinner daily 🚇 St. Clair

CAFÉ DIPLOMATICO ($)
Still not gussied up, it has mosaic marble floors, wrought iron chairs and a glorious cappuccino machine. A Toronto tradition on weekends.
➕ G7 ✉ 594 College Street ☎ 416/534-4637 🕐 Sun–Thu 8am–1am, Fri, Sat 8am–2am 🚋 College Street streetcar

ESPLANADE BIER MARKT ($)
A traditional Belgian-themed tile, wood-and-brick bistro where mussels and French fries are king. Over 100 bottled beers and more on tap, to enjoy with Flemish beef stew or wild boar sausages.
➕ K9 ✉ The Esplanade ☎ 416/862-7575 🕐 Daily 11am–1am 🚇 Union

FUTURE BAKERY ($)
European style stand-in-line cafeteria, beloved for its generous portions of goulash, cabbage rolls, beef borscht and schnitzel sandwiches.
➕ H6 ✉ 483 Bloor Street West ☎ 416/922-5875
🚇 Spadine or Bathurst

JUST DESSERTS ($)
Too much of a good thing is wonderful. Over 20 mouthwatering cakes, ten deep-dish pies, eight cheesecakes and a delectable assortment of cookies and tarts.
➕ K7 ✉ 555 Yonge Street (and other locations around the city) ☎ 416/963-8089 🕐 Daily 11am–1am
🚇 Wellesley

OVER EASY ($)
Champions of breakfast can enjoy dozens of egg dishes with double smoked bacon, smoked salmon, pancakes, home fries with onions, and more. Great coffee and French toast with caramelized bananas and Canadian maple syrup.
➕ J6 ✉ 208 Bloor Street West ☎ 416/922 2345 🕐 Daily 6am–4am 🚇 St. George or Museum

STARBUCKS WARS

Now that the coffee grounds have settled and the battle of the beans has stabilized into a cold war fought with iced Moccaccino, can you just get a regular cup of coffee anywhere? American-owned Starbucks goes head to head with locally owned Second Cup, and not too far behind it Timothy's World News Café. Lettieri is also a small chain with legions of fans. Second Cup is alive and inviting, with murals and individual ambience, and Timothy's offers plenty of reading material. Still a favorite is Tim Horton's for a light meal and great coffee.

Ethnic Excellence

TABLES WITH A VIEW

On the 54th floor of Mies van der Rohe's TDC, **Canoe** (➤ 67) offers a view of surrounding skyscrapers. At the top of the Park Plaza, the **Roof Restaurant** (✉ 4 Avenue Road ☎ 416/924-5471) and the adjacent lounge afford great views of downtown. **Scaramouche** (➤ 65) has window seats on the downtown skyline. The most stunning view of all is from **360** on top of the CN Tower (☎ 416/362-5411).

MIDDLE EASTERN/ MEDITERRANEAN

BOUJADI ($)

Brightly colored family-run café hung with rugs, brass and pottery. No dairy products. Try *tagines*, *pastilla* and *merguez* sausage. Honey pastries, mint tea, and dance entertainment on Saturdays.
➕ K2 ✉ 999 Eglinton Avenue West ☎ 416/440-0258 🕐 Dinner Tue–Sat 🚇 Eglinton

CHIADO ($$)

Reminiscent of a Lisbon bistro. Stick to such signature Portuguese dishes as the marinated sardines, poached salted cod and the *nato do céu*.
➕ F7 ✉ 864 College Street (at Concord Avenue) ☎ 416/538-1910 🕐 Lunch and dinner Mon–Sat 🚋 College Street streetcar

GRANO ($$)

A riotous celebration of rustic Italy. Tables are painted in brilliant mustard and cherry red, wine is served in tumblers and arias fill the air. The counter displays more than 50 antipasti. Pasta, meat and fish dishes change daily. Casual and fun.
➕ K2 ✉ 2035 Yonge Street ☎ 416/440-1986 🕐 Mon–Fri 10am–10.30pm, Sat 10am–11pm 🚇 Davisville

OLIVE & LEMON ($$)

Dishes are restrained yet exuberant. The arts and creative community love the sautéed olives and lemons with fresh bread. Plump grilled sardines, daily fish and meat and back-to-basics spaghetti and meatballs in a spare, storefront restaurant.
➕ H6 ✉ 119 Harbord Street ☎ 416/923-3188 🕐 Dinner daily 🚇 Spadina

OUZERI ($$)

Very Athens. Spirited, casual and crowded at night and on weekends. Exhaustive menu of appetizers and small plates of octopus, sardines with mustard, calamari, shrimp with feta and wine, plus traditional Greek dishes. Outdoor patio.
➕ N6 ✉ 500A Danforth Avenue ☎ 416/778-0500 🕐 Sun, Mon, Wed, Thu 11am–11pm, Tue, Fri, Sat 11am–2am 🚇 Danforth

ASIAN

EDO ($$)

A vast, intriguing menu prepared by an artist of sushi and sashimi. Grilled mushrooms and thickly sliced eggplant are baked to silken texture; soft shell crab and set menus for a balanced and exciting meal.
➕ J2 ✉ 484 Eglinton Avenue West ☎ 416/322-3033 🕐 Dinner daily 🚇 Eglinton West

EMA-TEI ($$)

Frequented by many Japanese visitors to Toronto because it delivers absolutely authentic cuisine, from the perfect appetizers to the fresh sushi.
➕ J8 ✉ 30 St. Patrick Street ☎ 416/340-0472 🕐 Lunch Mon–Fri; dinner daily 🚇 Osgoode

GOLDFISH ($$)

The facade is glass—it says come on in. You'll find a minimalist chic interior with a menu to match: the flavors of southeast Asia, the substance of Italian pasta and the honesty of vegetarian culture. And yet, a warm bowl of rice pudding with dried fruits is probably the best dessert.

➕ H6 ✉ 372 Bloor Street West ☎ 416/513-0077 🕐 Daily noon–10.30pm 🚇 Bathurst

LAI WAH HEEN ($$$)

A beautiful meeting place. The excellent food is prepared in a specially equipped Cantonese kitchen. Try the shark's fin soup, the abalone or one of the other extravagant dishes. There's a good *dim sum* menu too.

➕ J8 ✉ 110 Chestnut Street in the Metropolitan Hotel ☎ 416/977-9899 🕐 Lunch and dinner daily 🚇 Dundas or St. Patrick

MATA HARI ($)

Coconut-scented curries, really fresh fish enhanced by sauces spiced with lime leaf, chilis and red onion, spring rolls and satays, all served in a halogen-lit setting.

➕ J7 ✉ 39 Baldwin Street (off Spadina) ☎ 416/596-2832 🕐 Lunch Tue–Fri; dinner Tue–Sun 🚇 St. Patrick

NAMI ($$$)

Ultra-stylish and *very* expensive, this is frequented by Japanese business people and their guests. Prime attractions are the really fresh sushi and sashimi and darkly sophisticated interior.

➕ K8 ✉ 55 Adelaide Street East ☎ 416/362-7373 🕐 Lunch Mon–Fri; dinner Mon–Sat 🚇 Queen or King

TIGER LILY'S ($)

Down-to-earth and very reasonably priced noodle house. Lunch is served in a cafeteria format, at dinner there's table service. Vietnamese-style sweet-and-sour rice noodles served with the fish of the day is just one great choice.

➕ J8 ✉ 257 Queen Street West ☎ 416/977-5499 🕐 Lunch and dinner daily 🚇 Osgoode 🚋 Queen Street West streetcar

VANIPHA ($)

A hole-in-the-wall serving some of the best Laotian and Thai cuisine in the city, from pad Thai to grilled fish with tamarind sauce. Sticky-rice lovers should try it here.

➕ H7 ✉ 193 Augusta Avenue ☎ 416/340-0491 🕐 Lunch and dinner Mon–Sat 🚋 College Street streetcar

WAH SING ($)

A mealtime mecca, where the seafood tank is often filled with giant, queen crabs ready to sizzle with ginger and onion. Also worth looking out for the deep-fried oysters, duck with Peking sauce and, in season, two lobsters for the price of one.

➕ J7 ✉ 47 Baldwin Street ☎ 416/599-8822 🕐 Daily 11.30am–10.30pm 🚇 Dundas Westbound streetcar

AGE LIMIT

The legal drinking age in Ontario is 19, and young people should be prepared to show photo ID because entry and/or alcohol service can be refused.

Shopping Areas & Department Stores

TIMOTHY EATON

Timothy Eaton emigrated from Ireland in 1854 and set up shop in St. Mary's, Ontario. He arrived in Toronto in 1869 and opened a store on Yonge Street, where he started innovative merchandizing and marketing techniques, like fixed prices, cash-only sales, refunds and mail order—all unique then. Sadly, many stores have since closed and Eaton's is now part of the Sears Canada group.

THE BAY

Designer boutiques and a pleasant store to shop in. Take a break at SRO art-deco bar restaurant.

✚ J8 ✉ 176 Yonge at Queen ☎ 416/861-9111 🚇 Queen

BLOOR STREET

The Canadian flagship store Holt Renfrew is here, along with haute retail—Chanel, Tiffany, Hermès, Roots and Gap, Body Shop, Pottery Barn, Ashley Danier Leather and Benetton.

✚ J6–K6 🚇 Bloor-Yonge

COLLEGE PARK & ATRIUM ON BAY

The first is a more intimate, less hectic version of Eaton Centre with 100 stores; the second is even smaller with 60 stores.

✚ J7 🚇 College
✚ J6 🚇 Bay

EATON CENTRE

A million visitors a week shop in this vast indoor mall on three levels. Everything you've ever thought of is here.

✚ J8–K8 ✉ Yonge between Dundas and Queen 🚇 Dundas

HAZELTON LANES

A warren-like complex of over 85 stores with prestigious names—Gianni Versace, Valentino, Fogal, Turnbull & Asser, Rodier and Ralph Lauren. Lox, Stock and Bagel Deli opens to an appealing tree- and flower-filled courtyard for lunch in summer. Among the newest tennants is the giant Whole Foods Market, an all organic supermarket.

✚ J5–J6 🚇 Bay

HOLT RENFREW

Canada's answer to Harvey Nichols. Three floors of designer fashion, hairdressing salon, Estée Lauder Spa, perfumes and a café.

✚ J6 ✉ 50 Bloor Street West ☎ 416/922-2333 🚇 Bloor-Yonge

QUEEN STREET WEST

The hip shopping area where Canada's young designers rule. Fashions, antique clothing, flamboyant shoes, jewelry and household design.

✚ G8–J8 🚇 Osgoode

QUEEN'S QUAY

Tourist shopping spot on the waterfront with a variety of quality stores—from Rainmakers, featuring whimsical umbrellas and insulated rainwear, to Suitables, offering reasonably priced silk blouses.

✚ J9 🚇 LRT

ROOTS

The Canadian store *par excellence*. Started as a single store in 1973, Roots (▶ 78) is now an internationally recognized brand name. Branches all over the city.

YORKVILLE

The premier shopping area. Yorkville and Cumberland Avenues are lined with boutiques selling everything from jewelry at Silverbridge and Peter Cullman, to leather at Lanzi of Italy. Galleries and bookstores too.

✚ J6 🚇 Bloor-Yonge

Antiques & Collectibles

C.C.LAI
Exquisite Asian antiques fill this store—furniture large and small, plus porcelain, jade, jewelry and religious objects.
➕ J6 ✉ 9 Hazelton Avenue ☎ 416/928-0662 🚇 Bay

FIFTY ONE ANTIQUES
Specializes in 17th- and 18th-century furniture (Empire, Biedermeier and other styles), along with various decorative items: vases, lamps, carvings, European paintings and other accessories.
➕ J6 ✉ 21 Avenue Road ☎ 416/968-2416 🚇 Bay

MARK MCLAINE
A personal collection of eclectic pieces—from pine furnishings to French sconces and costume jewelry to ceramics and sculpture. Great browsing with prices ranging from Can$20 to thousands.
➕ J6 ✉ Hazelton Lanes ☎ 416/927-7972 🚇 Bay

MICHEL TASCHEREAU
There are wonderful objects in this idiosyncratic collection. Huge armoires share space with Canadian folk-art items, and a variety of china, glass and English furniture.
➕ J6 ✉ 176 Cumberland Street ☎ 416/923-3020 🚇 Bay

THE PAISLEY SHOP
This fine English furniture specialist also carries mirrors, porcelain, glass, cushions, lamps and lighting fixtures.
➕ J6 ✉ 77 Yorkville Avenue ☎ 416/923-5830 🚇 Bay

QUEEN'S TRADE CENTRE
This may not qualify as a high-end antiques store, but it is certainly a cherry-picker's delight. The space is jammed to the ceiling with all kinds of ephemera, from gas pumps to bicycles and neon beer signs to musical instruments.
➕ H8 ✉ 635 Queen Street West ☎ 416/504-6210 🚋 Queen Street West streetcar

R.A. O'NEILL
Country furniture from around the world—Germany, Britain, Holland and Ireland. You'll find tables, chairs, chests and cupboards, as well as decorative samplers and decoys.
➕ J5 ✉ 100 Avenue Road ☎ 416/968-2806 🚇 Bay

RED INDIAN AND EMPIRE ANTIQUES
An Aladdin's Cave full with objects dating from the 1930s to the 1950s. There's everything you could possibly imagine—Bakelite jewelry, neon signs, lighting of all sorts, Coca-Cola memorabilia and other retro items.
➕ H8 ✉ 536 Queen Street West ☎ 416/504-7706 🚋 Queen Street West streetcar

STANLEY WAGMAN
A major trader of period French furniture.
➕ J5 ✉ 224 Davenport Road ☎ 416/964-1047 🚇 Bay

TAX REFUNDS

Visitors can apply for a refund of GST (goods and services tax) on non-disposable items (➤ 91). The easiest way to secure the refund is to drop in at a duty-free shop on the way out of Canada. Fill out the forms, attach your receipts, and ask for the refund. Or you can mail your claim. For information contact Revenue Canada (➕ J5 ✉ Summerside Tax Centre, Summerside PE C1N 6C6 ☎ 902/432-5608).

Crafts & Jewelry

JEWELRY IN THE MAKING

At **18 Karat** (➕ J8 ✉ 71 McCaul Street in Village-by-the-Grange ☎ 416/593-1648), the craftspeople will copy any design that you wish. They will also repair or redesign antique settings. In Yorkville, shoppers can observe **Peter Cullman** fashioning beautiful pieces in his studio (➕ J5 ✉ 99 Yorkville Avenue in Cumberland Court ☎ 416/964-2196). Many items are inspired by natural and organic forms.

ALGONQUIANS SWEET GRASS GALLERY

Specializing in Native Canadian arts and crafts, the gallery is owned by an Ojibwa Indian and features Iroquois masks, porcupine quill boxes, Cowichan handknits from British Columbia, and much more.
➕ H8 ✉ 668 Queen Street West ☎ 416/703-1336 🚋 Queen Street West streetcar

BIRKS

A venerable Canadian name, selling jewelry, plus the best in china, crystal, silver, glass and other table accessories.
➕ J6 ✉ Manulife Centre, 55 Bloor Street ☎ 416/922-2266 🚇 Bay

DU VERRE

Brilliant glass pieces catch the eye here at one of the favorite shops on the Toronto bride's wedding list.
➕ G8 ✉ 188 Strachan Avenue ☎ 416/593-0182 🚋 Queen Street West streetcar

FRIDA CRAFT STORES

An appealing store to browse through, with Canadian crafts alongside items from Asia, Africa and Latin America. There are attractive fabrics, rugs, bags, costume jewelry and candles, as well as a variety of knick-knacks.
➕ K9 ✉ 39 Front Street East ☎ 416/366-3169 🚇 Union

GUILD SHOP

A prime place to purchase the latest and best in Canadian crafts including ceramics, glass, woodwork, jewelry and textiles by named artists, as well as Inuit and Native Canadian art.
➕ J6 ✉ 118 Cumberland Street ☎ 416/921-1721 🚇 Bay

LYNN ROBINSON

Avant-garde design. Wonderful *raku* (Japanese-type glazed earthenware) and bronze pieces plus contemporary glass, clay, wood and leather items by Canadian craftspeople.
➕ G8 ✉ 709 Queen Street West ☎ 416/703-2467 🚋 Queen Street West streetcar

PRIME GALLERY

Inspiring and appealing ceramic and other crafted objects, terra-cotta, fabric and jewelry—ranging in price from reasonable to very expensive.
➕ J8 ✉ 52 McCaul Street ☎ 416/593-5750 🚇 Osgoode

SILVERBRIDGE

Marvelously sculptured pieces of sterling silver. Necklaces, bracelets, rings and earrings for women, plus cuff links, money clips and key holders for men, all beautifully crafted. Prices range from Can$60 to $1,600.
➕ J6 ✉ 162 Cumberland Street ☎ 416/923-2591 🚇 Bay

SNOW LION INTERIORS

Worth seeking out for its selection of Asian crafts. You'll also find Tibetan rugs, plus a variety of ceramics, fabrics, lamps, jewelry, and more.
➕ K4 ✉ 575 Mount Pleasant Road ☎ 416/484-8859 🚇 St. Clair 🚋 Mount Pleasant streetcar

Books

ABELARD

A book lover's dream, offering a broad and well-cataloged selection of antiquarian and second-hand books. Armchairs for browsing in comfort.
➕ H8 ✉ 519 Queen Street West ☎ 416/504-2665
🚃 Queen Street West streetcar

THE COOKBOOK STORE

Every conceivable book for the cook and lover of food and wine is arranged here according to cuisine from Afghan to Zimbabwean. There are also technical books for professional restaurateurs and special events.
➕ K6 ✉ 850 Yonge Street at Yorkville Avenue ☎ 416/920-2665 🚇 Bloor-Yonge

DAVID MIRVISH

Son of the famous Ed (➤ 14), David is an art lover and his store reflects his passion. It is filled with volumes on sculpture, painting, architecture, ceramics, photography and other related subjects.
➕ G6 ✉ 596 Markham Street ☎ 416/531-9975 🚇 Bathurst

OMEGA CENTRE BOOKSTORE

This store stocks titles on every conceivable New Age subject, from astrology and tarot to numerology and runes.
➕ J6 ✉ 29 Yorkville Avenue ☎ 416/975-9086 🚇 Bloor

NEW BALLENFORD

Interior design, graphic arts and architecture are the specialties in this store.
➕ G6 ✉ 600 Markham Street ☎ 416/588-0800 🚇 Bathurst

NICHOLAS HOARE BOOKSHOP

A store that invites browsing, especially for the latest British publications. Staff love books and can answer every question. There's a fireplace and comfy sofa.
➕ K9 ✉ 45 Front Street East ☎ 416/777-2665 🚇 Union

PAGES

This store has a fine selection of small magazines and other offbeat literary publications, plus especially well-stocked sections in literature, design and the visual and performing arts.
➕ J8 ✉ 256 Queen Street West ☎ 416/598-1447
🚃 Queen Street West streetcar

THEATERBOOKS

As the name suggests, this shop specializes in the performing arts. There are books and magazines on all aspects of theater, film, opera and dance.
➕ J6 ✉ 11 St. Thomas Street ☎ 416/922-7175 🚇 Bloor-Yonge

TORONTO WOMEN'S BOOKSTORE

This specialist bookstore carries all kinds of non-fiction titles on women's history, sexuality and politics, as well as fiction of interest to women. It also stocks current magazines and journals relating to women's studies, scripts and criticism, and at the same time functions as a community center.
➕ H6 ✉ 73 Harbord Street ☎ 416/922-8744 🚇 Spadina

MAJOR CHAINS

According to **World's Biggest Bookstore** (➕ J/K7 ✉ 20 Edward Street ☎ 416/977-7009), if you can't find a book in their store, then it doesn't exist. With 17 miles (11km) of shelves and more than a million books in this flagship store, that could be true.
Cole's (➕ J8–J9 ✉ Royal Bank Plaza ☎ 416/865-0090) is only one of this chain's many well-stocked general bookstores. The two major Canadian chains, Indigo and Chapters, merged in 2001. They both offer vast well-organized stock, substantial discounts on bestsellers, and such creature comforts as lounge chairs and cafés.

Fashions & Retro

CANADA'S OWN

Check out current Canadian fashion talent by visiting Eaton's and the Bay, where they are grouped together. In the Bloor-Yorkville area you'll find Canada's best-known designer Alfred Sung; as well as Marilyn Brooks, a venerable mentor of the fashion scene; Nina Mdivani, for theatrical-style women's fashions; Vivian Shyu, for sophisticated but simple women's fashion; Lida Baday, for high-end fashion; Marisaa Minicucci, and Dominic Bellissimo, the leather king. Native Torontonian Franco Mirabelli has his own Portfolio store in Eaton Centre. Queen Street West is the domain of young designers: John Fluevog (shoes), Angi Venni, Robin Kay (New Age environmentally correct interior design and fashions) and Kingi Carpenter (groovy, hip fashions).

BULLOCH TAILORS

This is where the city's professional, political and military men traditionally come to be kitted out. Bespoke suits begin at Can$995.

📌 K8 ✉ 43 Colborne Street ☎ 416/367-1084 🚇 Union

CABARET

The place to buy period costume and retro fashions. Seek out velvet and sequined gowns or that perfect smoking jacket.

📌 H8 ✉ 672 Queen Street West (west of Palmerston) ☎ 416/504-7126 🚇 Osgoode 🚋 Queen Street West streetcar

CHANEL

Classic high fashion from the famous French name. This is one of only two boutiques in Canada. It carries Chanel's full line, plus accessories.

📌 J6 ✉ 131 Bloor Street West ☎ 416/925-2577 🚇 Bay or Bloor-Yonge

F/X

Outrageous fashions, including those by (eccentric) British trendsetter Vivienne Westwood, fill the racks at this hip store. Also on Spadina and Yorkville.

📌 H8 ✉ 515 Queen Street West ☎ 416/504-0888 🚋 Queen Street West streetcar

GEORGE BOURIDIS

Toronto's premier shirt-maker stocks more than 400 fabrics from all over the world. Custom-made shirts start at Can$185; a silk blouse will set you back at least Can$260.

📌 K8 ✉ 193 Church Street between Dundas and Shuter Street ☎ 416/363-4868 🚇 Dundas

HARRY ROSEN

Three floors of fashions for men including all the top men's designers—Armani, Valentino, Calvin Klein and Hugo Boss.

📌 J6 ✉ 82 Bloor Street West ☎ 416/972-0556 🚇 Bloor-Yonge or Bay

HOAX

Avant-garde fashion house producing innovative fashions for both men and women for almost 20 years. The prices are reasonable, given the fine quality.

📌 J6 ✉ 114 Cumberland Street ☎ 416/929-4629 🚇 Bay

I-CII

An unusual space inside the Courtyard. They carry the designs of Comme des Garcons, Junya Watanabe and Martina Margiela.

📌 J6 ✉ 99 Yorkville ☎ 416/925-3380 🚇 Bay or Museum

MAX MARA

Largest manufacturer and retailer of Italian high fashion. Contemporary, sophisticated looks with glamorous accessories.

📌 J6 ✉ 131 Bloor Street West ☎ 416/928-1884 🚇 Bay or Museum

STOLLERY'S

Long-established store with a distinct English flavor. Originally for men only, it now has women's clothes, from the likes of Austin Reed and Burberry.

📌 K6 ✉ 1 Bloor Street West ☎ 416/922-6173 🚇 Bloor-Yonge

Food & Housewares

ALL THE BEST FINE FOOD

Best breads, salads, entrées, jams, relishes, sauces and cheeses. Take a leaf out of the book of Rosedale's residents.

➕ K5 ✉ 1099 Yonge Street ☎ 416/928-3330 🚇 Rosedale

ARLEQUIN

The mouthwatering display will tempt you to put together a gorgeous picnic feast of pâtés, salads and pastries.

➕ J5 ✉ 134 Avenue Road ☎ 416/928-9521 🚇 Bay or St. George

DANIEL ET DANIEL

All kinds of foods can be purchased here—from a cappuccino and croissant for breakfast to pâtés, mini-pizzas, quiches, salads and hot and cold hors d'oeuvres for lunch.

➕ K7 ✉ 248 Carlton Street ☎ 416/968-9275 🚇 College 🚋 Carlton streetcar

DINAH'S CUPBOARD

A charmingly cluttered and inviting store. There are plenty of dishes that can help make a picnic, along with mini-meals you can heat up in the microwave.

➕ J6 ✉ 50 Cumberland Street ☎ 416/921-8112 🚇 Bloor-Yonge

EN PROVENCE

A beautiful store featuring household treasures from France—ceramics, table accessories and luxurious fabrics. The tablecloths, napkins and china are fabulous.

➕ J6 ✉ 20 Hazelton Avenue ☎ 416/975-9400 🚇 Bay

FORTUNE HOUSEWARES

This is the place to browse for top-of-the-line housewares that are sold at up to 20 percent off their normal price elsewhere. Brand-name cookware, plus utensils and every kind of kitchen gadget.

➕ H7 ✉ 388 Spadina Avenue ☎ 416/593-6999 🚇 Dundas 🚋 College streetcar, bus 77X

DINAH'S CUPBOARD

Dinah's prides themselves on sourcing the world's finest foods, such as raw-milk Quebec cheeses. The freshly baked breads and cakes are peerless and the selection of teas, coffees and spices is legend.

➕ J5 ✉ 50 Cumberland Street ☎ 416/921-8112 🚇 Bay

TEN REN TEA

In the center of Chinatown, this store stocks fine teas in urns and also sells such items as slimming tea and health-oriented infusions. You will also find stocks of tiny, eminently collectible Chinese teapots and teacups.

➕ H8 ✉ 454 Dundas Street West at Huron ☎ 416/598-7872 🚋 Dundas streetcar

TEUSCHER OF SWITZERLAND

This store offers an extraordinary range of chocolate—more than 100 different types in fact, including 20 or so truffles. They are handmade in Switzerland.

➕ J6 ✉ 55 Avenue Road in Hazelton Lanes ☎ 416/961-1303 🚇 Bay or St. George

PICNIC SPOTS

Toronto has so much green space that finding a picnic spot is not a problem. The best locations are some of the most obvious—The Toronto Islands, the lakefront at Harbourfront or further west at Sunnyside, the beach in The Beaches neighborhood, and High Park. Downtown, join the workers in Nathan Phillips Plaza or any of the grand spaces at the base of such towers as the TDC. Cumberland Park is an unusual city park featuring groves of indigenous trees, herbs, flowers and a megaton rock. It takes up a half of the block of Cumberland between Avenue Road and Belair.

77

Fun & Leisure

FOR MAGAZINE MANIACS

Great Canadian News Co.
(🛐 J9 ✉ BCE Place
☎ 416/363-2242), with its
2,000 magazines and 60
newspapers from around the
world, is a magazine lover's
paradise. **Maison de la
Presse Internationale** (🛐 J6
✉ 124 Yorkville Avenue
☎ 416/928-2328) stocks the
widest selection of foreign
publications.

CASABLANCA

This elegant store sells
premium Cuban and inter-
national cigars—Cohiba,
Bolivar, Montecristo and
Romeo & Julietta, for
example. Personal humidors,
pipes, cigarette cases and
lighters make good gifts for
diehard smokers.
🛐 K8 ✉ 4 King Street West
☎ 416/362-5722 🚇 King

CLUB MONACO

For casual, young fashions
there is nowhere better
than this chain, which has
several stores in the city.
This is the flagship store.
🛐 H8 ✉ 403 Queen Street
West ☎ 416/979-5633
🚃 Queen Street West streetcar

JOHN FLUEVOG

The most flamboyant
shoes you can imagine are
found at this ultra-hip
outlet. Madonna and
Paula Abdul have been
known to shop here.
🛐 J8 ✉ 242 Queen Street
West ☎ 416/581-1420
🚃 Queen Street West streetcar

KIDDING AWOUND

A collection of music
boxes and clockwork toys
to inspire adult nostalgia.
Fun items from the 1950s
to the '90s. If you can
wind it, it's here.
🛐 J9 ✉ 91 Cumberland Street
☎ 416/926-8996 🚇 Bay

OH YES, TORONTO

Yes, it deals in really bad-
taste souvenirs that shout
the city's name. They are
mostly good quality and
more attractive than
what's on offer elsewhere.
🛐 J8 ✉ Eaton's Centre
☎ 416/465-6354 🚇 Dundas

PETER FOX

Women who have ever
worn the shoes from this
Vancouver-based designer
love them for their excellent
fit and for their elegant and
Victorian-romantic design.
Satin or leather, they're
quite exquisite.
🛐 J6 ✉ 24 Bellair
☎ 416/960-5572 🚇 Bloor-
Yonge

ROOTS

Designs and sells fine-
quality leather jackets,
handbags, carrying cases,
shoes and boots. Wool
melton cloth and leather
outerwear (such as the
2000 Olympics jackets
worn by Prince Charles
and Princes William and
Harry) are renowned.
There's also Roots for
the home: upholstery,
wooden furniture,
bedding and a line of
toiletries and jewelry.
🛐 J6 ✉ 95 Bloor Street West
☎ 416/323-3289 🚇 Bay

TILLEY ENDURABLES

This store bears the name
of the man who developed
the famous "Tilley Hat,"
which can be used for a
variety of purposes out in
the wilderness. The store
also stocks a range of other
great outdoors gear,
including lightweight
underwear, waterproofs
and a multi-pocketed
jacket that is invaluable
for photographers. The
larger, flagship store is on
Don Mills Road.
🛐 J9 ✉ 207 Queen's Quay
West ☎ 416/203-0463
🚇 Union then LRT;
✉ 900 Don Mills Road
☎ 416/441-6141

Gifts & Miscellaneous

ASHLEY CHINA

It stocks all the great names, not only in china, but also in glass (Baccarat, Kosta Boda, Waterford). The goods are displayed elegantly in table settings or in wall cases.

✚ J6 ✉ 55 Bloor Street West ☎ 416/964-2900 ⓠ Bloor-Yonge

L'ATELIER GREGORIAN

This is a store for the devoted music lover. It contains a stunning collection of classical music and jazz CDs.

✚ J6 ✉ 70 Yorkville Avenue ☎ 416/922-6477 ⓠ Bloor-Yonge

DRAGON LADY COMIC SHOP

If you are looking for an unusual, reasonably priced gift, try here. It sells comics dating back to 1950, posters and back issues of *Life* magazine.

✚ G7 ✉ 609 College Street at University ☎ 416/536-7460 ⓠ College

THE GUILD SHOP

Fine Canadian crafts by Inuit, First Nations and local artisans. A vast selection of soapstone carvings, jewelry, leather, glass, pottery, wood and textiles.

✚ J6 ✉ 118 Cumberland Street ☎ 416/921-1721 ⓠ Bay or Yonge

ICE

A perennial favorite of celebrities, who love to browse the eclectic array of trinkets, which include Kate Spade paper products, Hard Candy and Urban Decay cosmetics, glitzy T-shirts and tank tops, costume jewelry and other trendy souvenirs.

✚ J6 ✉ 163 Cumberland Street ☎ 416/964-6751 ⓠ Bay

THE IRISH SHOP

A broad selection of gifts, fashions and books from Ireland. You can pick up a kilt, a shawl, some lace or an item of jewelry.

✚ J6 ✉ 150 Bloor Street West ☎ 416/922-9400 ⓠ Bay or Bloor-Yonge

LEGENDS OF THE GAME

Sports fans head here to purchase the shirt, hat or signed gear of their favorite team or player. Needless to say, it doesn't come cheap.

✚ J8 ✉ 322A King Street West ☎ 416/971-8848 ⓠ St. Andrew

ROTMAN HAT

This old store offers a great range of hats—feather-light panamas, jaunty derbies and so-called "grouser hats," as worn in the jungle.

✚ H7 ✉ 345 Spadina Avenue ☎ 416/977-2806 ⌷ Dundas or College streetcars, bus 77X

SCIENCE CITY

Here, you will find fossil specimens, chemistry kits, hologram watches and all kinds of science-oriented games and books. For the seriously scientific, there are also optical instruments, including telescopes.

✚ J6 ✉ 50 Bloor Street West in Holt Renfrew Centre ☎ 416/968-2627 ⓠ Bloor-Yonge

MUSEUM STORES

The Art Gallery of Ontario store (➤ 39) offers reproductions, posters, jewelry, ceramics, glass, fabrics and books. The Royal Ontario Museum's five stores (➤ 40) have similar lines, along with good replicas of museum pieces, including jewelry and toy soldiers. The George R. Gardiner Museum of Ceramic Art (➤ 41) has a fine selection of ceramic items, while the fabric selection at the Museum for Textiles (➤ 56) is truly exotic.

Classical Music, Dance & Theater

MAJOR VENUES

The city's major performing
arts venues include:

Massey Hall
✚ K8 ✉ 178 Victoria Street
☎ 416/593-4828

Hummingbird Centre
(formerly the O'Keefe Centre)
✚ K9 ✉ 1 Front Street East
☎ 416/872-2262

**St. Lawrence Centre for the
Arts**
✚ K9 ✉ 27 Front Street East
☎ 416/366-7723

Roy Thomson Hall
✚ J8 ✉ 60 Simcoe Street
☎ 416/593-4828

Toronto Centre for the Arts
✉ 5040 Yonge Street
☎ 416/ 870-8000

Premiere Dance Theatre
✚ J9 ✉ Queen's Quay
Terminal ☎ 416/973-4000

CLASSICAL MUSIC

CANADIAN OPERA COMPANY

The company was
formed in 1950, and
performs a season of six
productions between
September and April at
the Hummingbird Centre.
✚ K9 ✉ 227 Front Street East
☎ 416/363-6671 or 416/872-
2262 ⊜ Union

TAFELMUSIK

This internationally known
chamber group plays
baroque music on
authentic period instru-
ments at Massey Hall or at
Trinity/St. Paul's United
Church at 427 Bloor
Street.
✚ H6 ✉ 427 Bloor Street
West ☎ 416/964-6337
⊜ Spadina

TORONTO MENDELSSOHN CHOIR

The choir was founded in
1895, when it gave its first
performance at Massey
Hall. It performs the great
choral works of Bach,
Handel, Elgar and others,
as well as those of
Mendelssohn. A claim to
fame for the choir is that it
sang Handel's *Messiah* for
the soundtrack of the
Spielberg film *Schindler's
List*. It usually performs at
Roy Thomson Hall.
✚ J8 ✉ 60 Simcoe Street
☎ 416/598-0422 or 416/593-
4828 ⊜ St. Andrew

TORONTO SYMPHONY ORCHESTRA

The city's premier
symphony orchestra is over
80 years old and performs a
season at Roy Thomson

Hall with top guest artists.
In addition to its classical
repertoire it also plays
light popular music and
puts on a very well-
supported regular series of
outdoor summer concerts.
✚ J8 ✉ 60 Simcoe Street
☎ 416/593-4828 ⊜ St. Andrew

DANCE

Except for the National
Ballet, most companies
perform at the Premiere
Dance Theatre in Queen's
Quay.

DANNY GROSSMAN DANCE COMPANY

Born in San Francisco,
Danny Grossman became
a local favorite when he
began working with
Toronto Dance Theatre
in 1973, before founding
his own company in 1975.
Since then he has
choreographed some 30
original works exhibiting
social concern, wit, fun
and arresting physicality.
✚ H6 ✉ 425 Queen Street
West ☎ 416/408-4543
⊜ Osgoode

NATIONAL BALLET OF CANADA

A beloved national icon.
Founded by Celia Franca
in 1951, the company has
gained a golden inter-
national reputation for
itself, with such stars as
Karen Kain and Kimberly
Glasco. It performs a
fall-to-spring season at the
Hummingbird Centre that
includes classics and
modern pieces.
✚ K8 ✉ 470 Queen's Quay
West ☎ 416/345-9686; tickets
426/872-2262 ⊜ LRT

TORONTO DANCE THEATRE

This is the leading contemporary dance company in Toronto. Directed by Christopher House, the company performs energetic choreographic works set to often surprising music. Examples are the Handel *Variations* and Artemis *Madrigals*. The company's performance venue is the Premiere Dance Theatre at Queen's Quay.

✚ L7 ✉ 80 Winchester Street ☎ 416/973-4000 🚋 Carlton streetcar

THEATER

BUDDIES IN BAD TIMES THEATRE

Not only is this the premier gay theater in Canada, it has also nurtured many contemporary straight writers. Its reputation was built by Sky Gilbert. On the cutting edge, it always delivers theater that challenges social boundaries. Additional draws are Tallulah's Cabaret (very popular Fri and Sat) and the bar.

✚ K7 ✉ 12 Alexander Street ☎ 416/975-8555 🚇 College, Wellesley

CANADIAN STAGE COMPANY

A company that produces comedy, drama and musicals by international and Canadian authors. This is the company, for example, that brought the Broadway hit *Angels in America* to Toronto. Its home base is the St. Lawrence Centre for the Arts, and it also puts on free summer performances in High Park.

✚ L8 ✉ 26 Berkeley Street ☎ 416/368-3110 🚋 King Street East streetcar

FACTORY THEATRE

Dedicated to producing the works of new Canadian playwrights which are put on in two theaters. Many of the company's productions have been on international tours and have had some success abroad.

✚ H8 ✉ 125 Bathurst ☎ 416/504-9971 or 416/864-9971 🚋 Bathurst streetcar

TARRAGON THEATRE

Another long-lasting Canadian theater company devoted to producing Canadian works by now-famous playwrights such as Michael Ondaatje, Michel Tremblay and Judith Thompson. Off-Broadway productions sometimes arrive here too. Small and intimate.

✚ H4 ✉ 30 Bridgman Avenue ☎ 416/531-1827 🚇 Dupont

THEATRE PASSE MURAILLE

This is another company that nurtures contemporary Canadian playwrights. It produces innovative and provocative works by such figures as Daniel David Moses and Wajdi Mouawad. The theater has two stages, one catering for an audience of 220, the other for just 70.

✚ H8 ✉ 16 Ryerson Avenue ☎ 416/504-7529 🚋 Queen Street West streetcar or streetcar south from Bathurst

LANDMARK THEATERS

The grand **Elgin and Winter Garden theaters** (✉ 189–91 Yonge Street ☎ 416/872-5555) are built one on top of the other. The **Royal Alexandra Theatre** (✉ 260 King Street West ☎ 416/872-1212) is Toronto's beloved, 1907 baroque, red-and-gilt venue. A block away is the **Princess of Wales Theatre** (☎ 416/872-1212), built for *Miss Saigon* and decorated by Frank Stella. The **Canon Theatre** (✉ 244 Victoria Street ☎ 416/872-1212) is an historic plush theater with turn-of-the-century style and elegance.

81

Comedy, Dinner Theater & Film

EXPORTING LAUGHTER

Canadians are thought of as a staid bunch, compared with their neighbors to the south. Yet much of what Americans laugh at is either written or performed by Canadians—from *Saturday Night Live* and *SCTV* to *Spy Magazine* to *The Kids in the Hall*. Lorne Michaels, Earl Pomerantz, Dan Aykroyd, Wayne and Shuster, John Candy, Martin Short, Jim Carrey, Howie Mandel… Canadians have a great talent for irony and satire.

COMEDY

THE LAUGH RESORT
Up-and-coming comedy performers appear at this modestly priced venue.
✚ K8 ✉ 370 King Street West
☎ 416/364-5233 🚇 Queen

SECOND CITY
This venue is the source of many Canadian comedians who were to make it big in the US— John Candy, Dan Aykroyd, Bill Murray, Martin Short, and others.
✚ H9 ✉ 56 Blue Jays Way
☎ 416/343-0011 🚇 Union

YUKYUK'S
The other home of great Canadian comedy. Begun in the 1960s and modeled on similar theaters in New York and Los Angeles, this venue nurtured such Canadian stars as Jim Carrey, Harland Williams, Howie Mandel and Norm MacDonald. It has also hosted American comics Jerry Seinfeld, Robin Williams and Sandra Bernhard.
✚ K2 ✉ 2335 Yonge Street
☎ 416/967-6425 🚇 Eglinton

DINNER THEATER

FAMOUS PEOPLE PLAYERS DINNER THEATRE
This group specializes in a unique form of theater called black light theater. Black-clad players move around manipulating life-size puppets of famous people (such as Liberace or Barbra Streisand) and props. The bar was sponsored by the actor Paul Newman and the theater by Elton John. The troupe has had great success on Broadway in New York.
✚ F8 ✉ 110 Sudbury Street
☎ 416/532-1137 🚇 Queen streetcar to Dovercourt

MYSTERIOUSLY YOURS
The audience helps sleuth out the guilty party at this murder mystery, comedy showcase. There are dinner-and-show or show-only options.
✚ K2 ✉ 2026 Yonge Street
☎ 416/482-5200
🚇 Davisville (3 blocks north)

TOP OF THE SQUARE
This dinner theater produces several impressionist shows annually. It might feature An Evening at Les Cages, hosted by Joan Rivers. Expect plenty of audience participation.
✚ K8 ✉ 279 Yonge Street
☎ 416/364-5200 🚇 Dundas

FILM

CARLTON CINEMAS
This is one of the best places to see subtitled foreign films and cutting-edge North American independent films.
✚ K7 ✉ 20 Carlton Street
☎ 416/598-2309 🚇 College

CINÉMATHÈQUE ONTARIO
Organizes showings of directors' retrospectives, contemporary Canadian and international films, and documentaries. All the films are screened at the Art Gallery of Ontario.
✚ K7 ✉ 2 Carlton Street
☎ 416/967-7371 🚇 College

Live Music

FREETIMES CAFÉ

Go to hear the folk acoustic entertainment. Mondays is open house, so bring your instrument and sign up at 7pm.

✚ H7 ✉ 320 College Street between Major and Roberts ☎ 416/967-1078 🚃 College streetcar

HEALEY'S

Pictures of Jeff Healey with showbiz-friends Ron Wood and Jon Bon Jovi, and Queen Elizabeth line the walls of this banquette and sofa filled club.

✚ H8 ✉ 179 Bathurst Street ☎ 416/703-5882 Ⓜ Osgoode 🚃 Queen streetcar

HORSESHOE TAVERN

A sawdust-on-the-floor-type place, where The Police, The Band, Blue Rodeo and Barenaked Ladies got their start in Canada. Live rock 'n'roll Thursday to Saturday, country music Monday to Wednesday

✚ H8 ✉ 370 Queen Street West ☎ 416/598-4753 🚃 Queen Street West streetcar

LEE'S PALACE

Venue for the latest in rock music including up-and-coming British groups. Home to local alternative bands. Dance bar with DJ.

✚ H6 ✉ 529 Bloor Street West ☎ 416/532-7383 Ⓜ Bathurst

MONTREAL JAZZ CLUB

Long-standing jazz venue hosting international and local talent such as Marion McPartland, Carol Welsman Quartet and Memo Acevedo Quintet.

✚ K8 ✉ 65 Sherbourne Street ☎ 416/363-0179 🚃 King Street streetcar

ORBIT ROOM

Steeped in tradition of a classic cocktail lounge in the heart of Little Italy. Semi-circular booths, etched glass and a music line-up of the 1960s, R&B and blues.

✚ G7 ✉ 580A College Street ☎ 416/535-0613 🚃 College streetcar

PHOENIX CONCERT THEATRE

Patti Smith, Screaming Headless Torso and Smashing Pumpkins have played here. Dance on weekends in an Egyptian-Greek fantasy set.

✚ K7 ✉ 10 Sherbourne Street ☎ 416/323-1251 Ⓜ Wellesley or College

REX JAZZ AND BLUES BAR

This club offers a lineup of top local and up-and-coming modern jazz artists.

✚ J8 ✉ 194 Queen Street West ☎ 416/598-2475 🚃 Queen Street West streetcar

RIVOLI

Hip club-restaurant for an eclectic mix of grunge, blues, rock, jazz, cabaret and poetry reading.

✚ H8 ✉ 332 Queen Street West ☎ 416/532-1598 or 416/596-1908 Ⓜ Osgoode 🚃 Queen Street West streetcar

TOP O' THE SENATOR

Relax on the couches or the old cinema seats in this 1930s jazz/cabaret spot.

✚ K8 ✉ 249 Victoria Street ☎ 416/364-7517 Ⓜ Dundas

LOW-COST TICKETS & INFORMATION

Get day-of-performance half-price tickets at the TO Tix booths at Yonge and Dundas Streets inside the Eaton Centre (✚ K8 🕐 Tue–Sat noon–7.30 ☎ 416/536-6468). To find out what's on try *Toronto Life*, *Where Toronto* and the weekend editions of the *Globe & Mail*, *Toronto Star* and *Toronto Sun*. *Eye* or *Now* cover the hip scene, *Xtra!* the gay action.

Dance Clubs

CIGAR & POOL SCENES

Humidors have a major presence at **Black and Blue** (**+** J6 ✉ 150 Bloor Street ☎ 416/920-9900). Pool hustlers have endless choices including the huge, ultra comfortable **Academy of Spherical Arts** (**+** F9 ✉ 38 Hanna Avenue ☎ 416/532-2782) and the popular Bedford Ballroom (**+** J6 ✉ 232 Bloor Street West ☎ 416/966-4450).

THE DOCKS

Located right on the water, the Docks is every kind of nightlife action crammed into 41,000sq ft (3,813sq m). Dive into the newly renovated Deep End Nightclub and you'll see what a million dollars in sight and sound feels and looks like. When you're looking for a party, you'll be sure to find it at Tides Party Bar–billiards and large screen TVs that visually interact with the dance floor. The Aqua Lounge is a more intimate nightclub setting equipped with a separate dance floor and a great Toronto skyline view. Before hitting the clubs, dine at Stokers Patio, probably the most incredible patio restaurant . Other activities include karting, a golf driving range, volleyball, swimming pool, paintball range, drive-in and lots more.
+ L10 ✉ 11 Polson Street ☎ 416/461-DOCK 🚇 Union

BERLIN

Assorted sounds—Latin, hip-hop, top 40, R&B and house—attract a more sophisticated crowd to this comfortable club.
+ K2 ✉ 2335 Yonge Street ☎ 416/489-7777 🚇 Davisville

EL CONVENTO RICO

Famed for its weekend 1am drag shows. Lambada the night away until 4am.
+ J7 ✉ 750 College Street ☎ 416/588-7800 🚇 College 🚋 College streetcar west

CHICK 'N' DELI

The dance floor gets jammed at this youthful R&B spot. Refuel with chicken wings and barbecue dishes.
+ K2 ✉ 744 Mount Pleasant Road ☎ 416/489-3363 🚇 Eglinton

COURT HOUSE CHAMBER LOUNGE

In a gloriously reappointed historic court building. This celebrity favorite boasts 30-ft (9-m) ceilings and vintage mirrors, and spins old school classics for a hip professional-age crowd.
+ K8 ✉ 10 Court Street ☎ 416/214-9379 🚇 King

CROCODILE ROCK

Bar-restaurant and dance space that features slams on Saturday night. The crowd grooves to '70s and '80s dance sounds.
+ J8 ✉ 240 Adelaide Street West at Duncan ☎ 416/599-9751 🚇 St. Andrew

CUTTY'S HIDEAWAY

A mellow club on the Danforth where a Caribbean crowd sways to salsa and reggae.
+ N6 ✉ 538 Danforth Avenue ☎ 416/463-5380 🚇 Chester

EASY & THE FIFTH

An older crowd gathers in the loft-like space. The music leans more to the romantic and even allows for real conversation. Cigar bar with Oriental rugs and plush couches.
+ H8 ✉ 225 Richmond Street West ☎ 416/979-3000 🚇 Osgoode

FLUID LOUNGE

Good-looking and hip dressers gain entry to the "underwater-styled" venue to dance to the neo funk, industrial and other up-to-the-minute music. Check for celebrities.
+ H8 ✉ 217 Richmond Street West ☎ 416/593-6116 🚇 Osgoode

IVORY

Plush club for the fashionable 30-plus crowd. Saturday is most popular but Sunday is exotic Middle-Eastern night with Arabic music.
+ J6 ✉ 69 Yorkville ☎ 416/927-9929 🚇 Bay

TONIC

A specialized theatrical environment with freedom and movement in a fresh, modern context. The world's first ever multimedia light show; 72 TVs hover over a central dance space.
+ H8 ✉ 117 Peter Street ☎ 416/204-9200 🚇 Queen streetcar to Peter

Bars

AVENUE
Beautiful people, professional hockey players and visiting celebs are four-deep at the bar on weekends. Great martinis and a good bar menu.
✚ J6 ✉ Four Seasons Hotel, 21 Avenue Road ☎ 416/964-0411 🚇 Bay

BAR ITALIA
The slick spot in Little Italy for the young and the beautiful. Upstairs there's a plush pool area. Downstairs it's coffee, alcoholic drinks and Italian specialties all round.
✚ G7 ✉ 582 College Street ☎ 416/535-3621 🚋 College Street streetcar

C'EST WHAT
A cellar-style bar that's very casual and comfortable. You can relax and enjoy quiet conversation while you listen to whatever folk-acoustic group is playing.
✚ K9 ✉ 67 Front Street East ☎ 416/867-9499 🚇 Union

FIONN MACCOOL'S
In the heart of downtown, Fionn MacCool's features English and Irish beers on tap, and traditional foods like pies, pasties, coddles and fish and chips. Live Celtic music most nights attracts a Toronto microcosm of students, business people and those looking for a taste of home.
✚ K9 ✉ 35 The Esplanade (corner of Church and The Esplanade) ☎ 416/362-2495 🚇 Union

ORBIT ROOM
This agreeable little bar is a haunt of local professional people, who like to gather upstairs. Comfortable, old-fashioned atmosphere, with semi-circular banquettes and etched glass. Entertainment provided by local groups.
✚ G7 ✉ 580A College Street ☎ 416/535-0613 🚋 College Street streetcar

ROTTERDAM
This is the place for serious beer drinkers—Bavarian-style beers and ales are brewed in huge tanks. About ten brews are on tap. It gets crowded later in the evening. Good summer patio.
✚ H8 ✉ 600 King Street West (at Portland) ☎ 416/504-6882 🚋 King Street streetcar

SOUZ DAL
A small hideaway with a Moroccan atmosphere including a copper bar and kilim wall hangings. The inviting candlelit patio under a trellis is a romantic spot to indulge in fruit-flavored martinis on summer evenings.
✚ G7 ✉ 636 College Street ☎ 416/537-1883 🚋 College Street streetcar

WAYNE GRETZKY'S
A shrine to the Canadian hockey player. Forget the food and head upstairs to the rooftop outdoor patio, which has great views out over the gardenias. Memorabilia decorate the long bar downstairs.
✚ H9 ✉ 99 Blue Jays Way ☎ 416/979-7825 🚇 St. Andrew

GAY TORONTO

To get a fix on the scene, pick up *Xtra!* or go to **Gay Liberation Bookstore/Glad Day Bookshop** (✚ K6 ✉ 598a Yonge Street ☎ 416/961-4161).
Among the long-standing popular bars are **Woody's** (✚ K7 ✉ 467 Church Street ☎ 416/972-0887); **The Barn/The Stables** (✚ K7 ✉ 418 Church Street ☎ 416/977-4702); **Pints** (✚ K7 ✉ 518 Church Street ☎ 416/921-8142), where the patio is jammed in summer; and **Tallulah's Cabaret** (✚ K7 ✉ 12 Alexander Street ☎ 416/975-8555) is the place to flaunt yourself and your dance technique to alternative music. Friday is supposedly women's night.

Luxury Hotels

HOTEL PRICES

Expect to pay the following prices per night for a double room, but it's always worth asking when you make your reservation whether any special deals are available.

Budget   up to Can$80
Mid-Range   up to Can$140
Luxury   over Can$200

COUNTRY LUXURY

For a languorous country-house experience convenient for Stratford (► 20), book a room at Langdon Hall. Built in 1902, it stands in 200 acres with superb accommodations set around a cloister garden. The main house has a lovely dining room and conservatory. Facilities include outdoor pool, tennis court, croquet lawn, billiards room, spa-fitness center and cross-country ski trails.
✉ RR 3, Cambridge, ON N3H 4R8 ☎ 519/740-2100

FOUR SEASONS

In the center of Yorkville, this is the city's top hotel. The service is personal yet unobtrusive, the 380 rooms spacious, elegant, comfortable and well equipped, and the facilities excellent. It has a world-class restaurant, Truffles (► 65), a great bar, Avenue (► 85), and the Studio Café attracts a celebrity crowd.
➕ J6 ✉ 21 Avenue Road ☎ 416/964-0411; fax 964-2301; www.fourseasons.com ⊗ Bay

INTERCONTINENTAL

With 209 rooms, this hotel around the corner from Yorkville provides personal service. Spacious rooms with Louis XVI-style furnishings offer every comfort. Signatures bar is a favorite rendezvous for afternoon tea or cocktails.
➕ J6 ✉ 220 Bloor Street West ☎ 416/960-5200; fax 960-8269; www.toronto.intercontinental.com ⊗ St. George

METROPOLITAN

A challenger to the Four Seasons in terms of its restaurants, which are celebrated for their cuisine and character; service is less splendid. The 425 modern rooms are equipped with the latest technology.
➕ J8 ✉ 108 Chestnut Street ☎ 416/977-5000; fax 977-9513; www.metropolitan.com ⊗ St. Patrick

PARK HYATT

The stylish 346 rooms have been renovated to an exceptional standard with fine fabrics and furnishings

and the latest in amenities. There are three restaurants and a still-water spa. The 299 rooms.
➕ J6 ✉ 4 Avenue Road ☎ 416/924-5471 or 800/778-7477; fax 924-4933; www.hyatt.com ⊗ Bay or Museum

ROYAL MERIDIEN KING EDWARD

An architectural jewel in marble and sculpted stucco. The Victoria Room is a favorite gathering place. The 299 rooms are very spacious, handsomely decorated and well equipped.
➕ K8 ✉ 37 King Street East ☎ 416/863-9700; fax 367-5515; www.lemeridien-kingedward.com ⊗ King

SUTTON PLACE

This hotel has seen some ups and downs over the years, but is back on form. Restaurant and bar, fitness facilities, indoor pool and sundeck, and a business center. 294 rooms.
➕ J6–J7 ✉ 955 Bay Street ☎ 416/924-9221 or 800/268-3790; fax 924-1778; www.suttonplace.com ⊗ Museum or Wellesley

WESTIN HARBOUR CASTLE

Large hotel hosting many conventions in a lakefront location; many of the 980 rooms have a lake view. The excellent facilities include Toula, for fine Italian dining, squash and tennis courts and an indoor pool.
➕ K9 ✉ 1 Harbour Square ☎ 416/869-1600 or 800/228-3000; fax 361-7448; www.westin.com/harbourcastle ⊗ Union

Mid-Range Hotels

DELTA CHELSEA

Large (1,591 rooms) but well-run, with excellent facilities for children.
🏨 J7 ✉ 33 Gerrard Street West ☎ 416/595-1975 or 800/243-5732; fax 585-4375; www.deltachelsea.com 🚇 College

FAIRMONT ROYAL YORK

Rooms vary and the service can be stretched as there are 1,365 rooms. Nine bars and restaurants—the Library Bar is noted for its martinis. Pool.
🏨 J9 ✉ 100 Front Street West ☎ 416/368-2511 or 416/863-6333 (reservations only); fax 860-5008; www.fairmont.com 🚇 Union

HILTON TORONTO

Near the Convention Center; 601 rooms over 32 floors. Indoor/outdoor pool.
🏨 J8 ✉ 145 Richmond Street West ☎ 416/869-3456 or 800/445-8667; fax 869-3187; www.hilton.com 🚇 Osgoode

MARRIOTT EATON CENTRE

Conveniently located, with 459 well-equipped rooms, a rooftop pool and a great steakhouse, JW's.
🏨 J8 ✉ 525 Bay Street ☎ 416/597-9200; fax 597-9211; www.marriotteatoncentre.com 🚇 Dundas

RADISSON PLAZA HOTEL ADMIRAL

Harbourfront hotel with rooftop pool, bar and terrace. The 157 rooms are well furnished and equipped. Squash court, two restaurants and a bar.
🏨 J9 ✉ 249 Queen's Quay West ☎ 416/203-3333 or 800/333-3333; fax 203-3100; www.radisson.com/torontoca_admiral 🚇 Union then LRT

RENAISSANCE TORONTO AT SKYDOME

Out of 346 functional rooms, 70 overlook the baseball turf. Pool, fitness center and squash courts.
🏨 H9 ✉ 1 Blue Jays Way ☎ 416/341-7100; fax 341-5091; www.renaissancehotels.com 🚇 Union

SHERATON

One of the city's largest hotels (1,377 rooms) with efficient service. Six restaurants/bars and a theater.
🏨 J8 ✉ 123 Queen Street West ☎ 416/361-1000; fax 947-4874; www.sheratoncentretoronto.com 🚇 Osgoode

WESTIN PRINCE

Set in 15 acres (6ha), 20 minutes from downtown in the Don Valley. The 381 rooms are serene. Katsura restaurant has excellent sushi and *robata* bars, tempura counter and teppanyaki-style cuisine. Putting green, tennis courts and fitness center.
🏨 Off map to northeast ✉ 900 York Mills Road, Don Mills ☎ 416/444-2511; fax 444-9597; www.toronto.com/westinprince 🚇 York Mills

WYNDHAM BRISTOL PLACE

One of the best hotels on the airport strip. The 287 rooms are well furnished and equipped. Pools and fitness facilities.
🏨 Off map to northwest ✉ 950 Dixon Road ☎ 416/675-9444; fax 675-4426; www.wyndham.com/hotels 🚇 Kipling

BED & BREAKFAST

Several bed-and-breakfast organizations help visitors to find rooms in private homes from Can$70 to Can$120 a night.

Toronto Bed & Breakfast
✉ Box 269, 253 College Street, ON M5T 1R5 ☎ 705/738-9449

Downtown Toronto Association of Bed-and-Breakfast Guesthouses
✉ Box 190, Station B, ON M5T 2W1 ☎ 416/368-1420

Budget Hotels

DORMS AND HOSTELS

In summer, university dorms provide fine budget accommodations. **Neil Wycik** (🏨 K7 ✉ 96 Gerrard Street East ☎ 416/977-2320; fax 977-2809) and **Victoria University** (🏨 J6 ✉ 140 Charles Street West ☎ 416/585-4524; fax 585-4530) are both conveniently located downtown. Other accommodations can be found at **University of Toronto** in Scarborough (☎ 416/287-7356; fax 287-7323). There are comfortable rooms and decent facilities (TV lounge, kitchen and laundry) at the downtown hostel (🏨 K8 ✉ 76 Church Street at King ☎ 416/971-4440; fax 971-4088). **Global Village Backpackers** (✉ 460 King Street West ☎ 416/703-8540; fax 416/703-3887; www.globalbackpackers.com) are Toronto's largest international-travelers' hostel, with 200 beds. Located in the downtown core, just a five-minute walk from the CN Tower, they offer shared facilities and a great atmosphere for students and youth travelers.

BOND PLACE

Established 286-room hotel. Restaurant and lounge.
🏨 K8 ✉ 65 Dundas Street East ☎ 416/362-6061; fax 360-6406; www.bondplacehoteltoronto.com 🚇 Dundas

COMFORT INN DOWNTOWN

Only two blocks south of Bloor, this 110-room hotel has large rooms and a restaurant. Access to nearby health club for a fee.
🏨 K6 ✉ 15 Charles Street East ☎ 416/924-1222; fax 927-1369; www.toronto.com/comfortdowntown 🚇 Bloor-Yonge

DAYS INN

Next door to Maple Leaf Gardens, this modern high-rise hotel has 536 reasonably priced rooms, sports bar, restaurant and an indoor pool.
🏨 K7 ✉ 30 Carlton Street ☎ 416/977-6655; fax 977-2865; www.toronto.com/daysinntoronto 🚇 College

HOLIDAY INN ON KING

Modern well-equipped rooms (425) at a good price for the location (opposite the Convention Centre). Downstairs restaurant-bar.
🏨 H8 ✉ 370 King Street West at Peter ☎ 416/599-4000; fax 599-7394; www.hiol.com 🚇 St. Andrew

HOWARD JOHNSON'S HOTEL, SELBY

In a handsome Victorian building, this relaxed midtown hotel is good value. Sixty-seven high-ceilinged rooms are individually decorated and furnished. Access to health club nearby for a fee.
🏨 K6 ✉ 592 Sherbourne ☎ 416/921-3142; fax 923-3177; www.toronto.com/selby 🚇 Sherbourne

HOTEL VICTORIA

In the financial district with only 48 small rooms. Some have coffeemakers and mini-refrigerators. Restaurant and lounge.
🏨 K9 ✉ 56 Yonge Street ☎ 416/363-1666; fax 363-7327; www.hotelvictoria-toronto.com 🚇 King

QUALITY HOTEL DOWNTOWN

Not far from the heart of the financial district, with 196-room modern rooms.
🏨 K8 ✉ 111 Lombard Street between Adelaide and Richmond ☎ 416/367-5555; fax 367-3470 🚇 King or Queen

STRATHCONA

Decent, if small, rooms at a fraction of the price of the Royal York right opposite. Coffee shop/restaurant and sports bar. Eighty-two rooms.
🏨 J9 ✉ 60 York Street ☎ 416/363-3321; fax 363-4679; www.thestrathcomahotel.com 🚇 Union

HOWARD JOHNSON'S INN, YORKVILLE

Great Yorkville location and good value with very reasonably priced modern rooms (there are only 71, so make a reservation). No additional facilities.
🏨 J5 ✉ 89 Avenue Road ☎ 416/964-1220; fax 964-8692; www.hojo.com 🚇 Bay or St. George

TORONTO
travel facts

ESSENTIAL FACTS

Customs regulations

- Visitors over 18 may bring in free of duty up to 50 cigars, 200 cigarettes and 1kg of tobacco; 1.14 liters of spirits or wine may be imported by travelers over the minimum drinking age of the province to be visited (19 in Ontario). You may bring in gifts up to Can$60.
- No firearms, plants or meats may be imported.
- Information from Revenue Canada ✉ 875 Heron Road, Ottawa, ON KIA OL8 ☎ 416/973-8022

Electricity

- 110v, 60Hz AC. American-style flat 2-pin plugs.

Lavatories

- Public lavatories are rare; use the ones provided in major shopping complexes and hotel lobbies, bars and restaurants.

Money matters

- Most banks have automatic teller machines (ATMs) that are linked to Cirrus, Plus or other networks and this is the easiest way to secure cash. However, before you leave check that your PIN number is valid in Canada. Also check on frequency and amount limits of withdrawals. For ATM locations look on the following websites: Matercard at www.mastercard.com or Visa/Plus at www.visa.com.
- Credit cards are widely accepted. American Express, Diner's Club, Discover, MasterCard and Visa are the most common.
- Traveler's cheques are accepted in all but small shops as long as the denominations are small ($20 or $50). If you carry traveler's checks

in Canadian dollars, you save on conversion fees.

National holidays

- 1 January, Good Friday and/or Easter Monday, Victoria Day (third Monday in May), Canada Day (1 July), Civic Holiday (first Monday in August), Labour Day (first Monday in September), Thanksgiving (second Monday in October), Remembrance Day (11 Nov), Christmas Day (25 Dec) and Boxing Day (26 Dec)

Opening hours

- Banks: generally Mon–Thu 10–3, Fri 10–6.
- Museums: hours vary.
- Shops: generally Mon–Wed 9.30 or 10–6, Sat, Sun 10–5. Hours are also often extended on Thu or Fri until 8 or 9.

Places of worship

- Baptist: Rosedale Baptist Church ✉ 877 Yonge Street ☎ 416/926-0732
- Episcopal: St. James' Cathedral ✉ 65 Church Street, at King ☎ 416/364-7865
- Islam: Toronto and Region Islamic Congregation ✉ 99 Beverley Hills Drive ☎ 416/245-5675
- Jewish: Beth Shalom Synagogue (Conservative), Holy Blossom Temple (Reform) ✉ 1445 Eglinton Avenue West ☎ 416/783-6103
- Presbyterian: St. Andrew's ✉ 75 Simcoe Street ☎ 416/593-5600
- Roman Catholic: St. Michael's Cathedral ✉ 200 Church Street ☎ 416/364-0234

Safety

- Toronto is considerably safer than most North American cities, but there is always danger of theft, and visitors need to exercise some caution in crowded areas and on the subway. Use common sense.

- Downtown, avoid Moss Park and don't enter Allan Gardens or High Park at night.

Smoking

- Smoking is banned in all public buildings, except in clearly designated smoking areas. All bars and restaurants are non-smoking zones.

Student travelers

- An International Student Identity Card (ISIC) reduces admission at some museums, theaters and other attractions.
- Always carry a photo ID to prove your age so you won't be excluded from bars and clubs.

Taxes

- The provincial retail sales tax is 8 percent; there is also a 5 percent tax on hotel/motel rooms and a national goods and services tax (GST) of 7 percent.
- Non-residents can apply for a refund of taxes on non-disposable merchandize that is taken out of the country within 60 days of purchase (► 73). Meals and restaurant charges, car rental, hotel accommodations and similar services do not qualify for the rebate.
- Information from Visitor Rebate Programme ✉ Revenue Canada, Summerside Tax Centre, Summerside PE C1N 6C6 ☎ 902/432-5608

Tipping

- As a rule, tip around 15 percent in restaurants and bars, 15–20 percent to cab drivers, Can$1 per bag to porters and Can$1 to a valet parking attendant. Hairdressers also expect 15–20 percent.

Visitors with disabilities

- Much of the city has been built in the last 20 years and many buildings are barrier free and well equipped with lifts for easy wheelchair access.
- For more detailed information, Disabled Information on Community Services ✉ Community Information Centre of Metropolitan Toronto, 425 Adelaide Street West, Toronto, ON M5V 3C1 ☎ 416/392-0505 🕐 Daily 8am–10pm

Women travelers

- Women will find Toronto hospitable and relatively safe (but see Safety opposite).
- For books and information stop by the Toronto Women's Bookstore ✉ 73 Harbord Street at Spadina ☎ 416/922-8744 🕐 Daily from 10.30 on weekdays, from noon Sun

GETTING AROUND

Underground and buses

- The subway consists of two lines –Bloor–Danforth and Yonge–University–Spadina. The first runs east–west from Kipling Avenue in the west to Kennedy Road in the east, where it connects with Scarborough Rapid Transit. The second runs from Finch Avenue in the north to Union Station, where it loops north along University Avenue connecting with the Bloor Line at St. George before proceeding to Wilson Avenue.
- Discounts are available for students 19 and under , senior citizens and for children under 12.
- To save money you can purchase ten tokens for a reasonable reduction in the cost per journey. Day, monthly and annual passes are also available.
- The subway system is connected to the bus and streetcar network. It is always wise to pick up a transfer at the

subway station from the push-button machine at the entrance or from the bus driver. By so doing, you can board a streetcar going east or west from the subway station if you need to, or transfer from the bus to the subway without paying extra.

- The subway operates Mon–Fri 6am–1.30am and Sun 9am–1.30am. A Blue Night Network is in operation outside those hours on basic surface routes, running about every 30 minutes.
- Be warned—bus stops are not always easy to see.
- From Union Station a Light Rapid Transit (LRT) line operates to Harbourfront, stopping between Queen's Quay and Rees Street. No transfer is needed to ride the LRT.
- For transit information pick up a Ride Guide at a subway station or call ☎ 416/393-4636 (7am–10pm)

Taxis
- The light on the rooftop will be turned on if the taxi is available.
- All taxis must display rates and contain a meter.
- Tip 15–20 percent.
- For more information on getting around ➤ 7.

MEDIA & COMMUNICATIONS

Telephones
- To dial outside the Toronto area codes of 416 or 905 add the prefix 1.
- To avoid hefty hotel surcharges on local calls use payphones, which are available everywhere.
- For long distance use AT&T, MCI or Sprint rather than calling direct. Access codes and instructions are found on your phone card. If they don't work, dial the operator and ask for the access code in Canada.
- To call the UK from Toronto dial 01144 and drop the first "0" from the number. To call the US from Toronto dial direct dial #1 plus the area code.

Post offices
- Postal services can be found at convenience and drugstores. Look for a sign in the window advertising postal services.
- There are also post office windows open in major shopping complexes like Atrium on the Bay ➕ J7–J8 ☎ 416/506-0911 Commerce Court ➕ J8–J9 ☎ 416/956-7452 Toronto Dominion Centre ➕ J8–J9 ☎ 416/360-7105 and First Canadian Place ➕ J8 ☎ 416/364-0540

Newspapers and Magazines
- There are four local dailies: the *Globe & Mail* and the *National Post*, which are the heavyweights, and the *Toronto Star* and *Toronto Sun*. There are also free papers like *Eye* and *Now*, essential for arts/entertainment listings, and *Xtra!* for its gay listings. There are also ethnic newspapers serving local communities.
- *Toronto Life* is the major monthly magazine. *Where Toronto* is usually provided free in your hotel room.

International newsagents
- The main chains selling international newspapers are Great Canadian News Co, with a number of outlets in town, and the Maison de la Presse Internationale ✉ 124 Yorkville Avenue ☎ 416/928-2328

Radio
- CBC Radio offers assorted programing from serious talk and

Ottakar's Branch List

Inside the M25

- Barnet
- Bromley
- Clapham Junction
- Enfield
- Epsom
- Greenwich
- Harrow
- Putney
- Science Museum
- Staines
- Walthamstow
- Wood Green

England

- Andover
- Ashford
- Banbury
- Barnstaple
- Barrow-in-Furness
- Basildon
- Basingstoke
- Bishop's Stortford
- Boston
- Bracknell
- Brentwood
- Bromsgrove
- Burton-on-Trent
- Bury St. Edmunds
- Camberley
- Carlisle
- Chatham
- Chelmsford
- Cheltenham
- Chippenham
- Cirencester
- Coventry
- Crawley
- Crewe
- Darlington
- Dorchester
- Eastbourne
- East Grinstead
- Eastleigh
- Fareham
- Farnham
- Folkestone
- Gloucester
- Grimsby
- Guildford
- Harrogate
- Hastings
- Haywards Heath
- Hemel Hempstead
- Hexham
- High Wycombe
- Horsham
- Huddersfield
- Kendal
- King's Lynn
- Lancaster
- Lincoln
- Loughborough
- Lowestoft
- Luton
- Lymington
- Maidenhead
- Market Harborough
- Milton Keynes
- Newton Abbot
- Northallerton
- Norwich
- Oldham
- Ormskirk
- Petersfield
- Poole
- Portsmouth
- Redhill
- St. Albans
- Salisbury
- Sheffield, Meadowhall
- Slough
- Southend
- Stafford
- Stevenage
- Sunderland
- Sutton
- Sutton Coldfield
- Tenterden
- Tiverton
- Trowbridge
- Truro
- Tunbridge Wells
- Wakefield
- Walsall
- Wells
- Weston-super-Mare
- Wilmslow
- Windsor
- Witney
- Woking, Peacocks Centre
- Woking, Wolsey Walk
- Worcester
- Yeovil

Scotland

- Aberdeen
- Aviemore
- Ayr
- Dumfries
- Dundee
- East Kilbride
- Edinburgh, Cameron Toll
- Edinburgh, George Street
- Elgin
- Falkirk
- Glasgow, Buchanan Galleries
- Inverness
- Kirkcaldy
- Newton Mearns
- Oban
- Peterhead

Wales

- Abergavenny
- Aberystwyth
- Carmarthen
- Llandudno
- Newport, Gwent

The islands

- Douglas, Isle of Man
- Newport, Isle of Wight
- St. Helier, Jersey
- St. Helier (de Gruchy), Jersey

Ottakar's Plc Registered Number: 2133199 VAT No: 561 9972 00
Registered Office: 72 St John's Road • Clapham Junction • London • SW11 1PT

OTTAKAR'S

drama to classical and other music as well as news. It broadcasts on 94.1 FM and 740 AM.

- Broadcasting in 30 different languages, CHIN at 100.7 FM and 1540 AM puts visitors in touch with the ethnic/multi-cultural scene.

Television

- Hotels usually receive all the channels available to cable subscribers. This includes CBC along with the major American networks like PBS, plus CNN and other cable stations such as Much Music, Toronto's version of MTV produced by Citytv.

EMERGENCIES

Emergency phone numbers

- Fire, police and ambulance ☎ 911
- Metro police station ✉ 40 College Street ☎ 416/808-2222
- Rape Crisis ☎ 416/597-8808
- Victim Assault ☎ 416/863-0511

Embassies and Consulates

- All embassies are in the national capital Ottawa.
- The following consulates are found in Toronto:
- UK ✉ 777 Bay Street at College ☎ 416/593-1267
- Australia ✉ 175 Bloor Street East ☎ 416/323-1155
- USA ✉ 360 University Avenue ☎ 416/595-1700

Lost property

- For articles left on a bus, streetcar or subway, TTC Lost Articles Office ✉ Bay Street subway station ☎ 416/393-4100 ◷ Mon–Fri 8–5
- If you lose a credit card or travelers' checks, report the loss immediately to the credit card company or the company issuing

the checks, and to the local police. Main international credit card phone numbers:
American Express ☎ 336/393-1111 (reverse charges);
Diner's Club ☎ 1/800/234-6377;
MasterCard ☎ 1/800/826-2181;
Visa ☎ 1/800/336-8472

Medical and dental treatment

- 24-hour emergency service is provided by the Toronto General Hospital ☎ 416/340-3111. The main entrance is at 200 Elizabeth Street, another entrance is at 150 Gerrard Street West.
- If you need a doctor, enquire at your hotel or seek a referral from the College of Physicians and Surgeons ✉ 80 College Street ☎ 416/961-1711 ◷ 9–5
- In the event of a dental emergency ask for a referral from the Ontario Dental Association ☎ 416/922-3900

Medicines

- Always bring a prescription for any medications in case of loss and also to show to the customs officers if necessary.
- Shopper's Drug Mart ✉ 360 Bloor Street West stays open daily until midnight. Several downtown locations are open 24 hours. Pharma Plus ✉ 68 Wellesley Street at Church ☎ 416/924-7760 is also open until midnight.

VISITOR INFORMATION

- You can obtain information from: Tourism Toronto ✉ 207 Queen's Quay West, suite 590, in the Queen's Quay Terminal ☎ 416/203-2500 or 800/363-1990 ◷ Summer: Mon–Thu 8.30–8, Fri 8.30–5, Sat 9–5, Sun 9.30–5. Winter: Mon–Fri 8.30–5 The visitor information centre in Eaton Centre is open daily.

Index